MW00811026

Pearls Hang in Dark Clouds

Pearls Hang in Dark Clouds

A Journey on a Long and Winding, Broken Road

LAWREN DELASS

RESOURCE *Publications* • Eugene, Oregon

PEARLS HANG IN DARK CLOUDS
A Journey on a Long and Winding, Broken Road

Resource Publications
An Imprint of Wipf and Stock Publishers
199 W. 8th Ave., Suite 3
Eugene, OR 97401

www.wipfandstock.com

PAPERBACK ISBN: 978-1-6667-4229-9
HARDCOVER ISBN: 978-1-6667-4230-5
EBOOK ISBN: 978-1-6667-4231-2

*"Forgiveness is the fragrance
the violet sheds on the
heel that has crushed it."*
Mark Twain

♦ Pearls Hang in Dark Clouds ♦

===

A Poem Written in Childhood

Oh, Grandmother, Oh, Grandmother	1967	3

First Three Poems Written as Teenager

I Would Love	1975	7
Young Maiden's Folly of the Senses	1976	8
Locked Up & Twisted	1977	9

Beyond

The Rose	1978	13
Ye Olde Love Poem	1978	14
Ride the Wave	1979	15
Charcoals & Rust	1979	16
Over Yonder Hills	1979	17
Rain	1979	18
Autumn's Inner Wind	1979	19
Pinch of Country	1980	20
Dead Tomatoes	1980	21
Oh, Great Shepard	1980	21
Fantasy ship	1980	22
Indiscreet	1980	23

Old Spiritual Poems by Various Authors | 1900 ~ 1921
Edited, Restored, and Reconstructed by Lawren DeLass

Are All The Children In?	Elizabeth Rosser	27
Conversion	Ophelia G. Adams	28
The Ninety & Nine	Ethel M. Colson	30
Dat Lil' Brack Sheep		

Beyond part two

A Yaqui Dream of Power	1980	35
The Dawn of Eve	1980	36
The Queen's Dusky Jewels	1980	37
Pink Poppies	1980	38
The City is Dying	1981	41
The Zoo Lion	1981	42
Little Big Head	1981	43
Lost Little Babe	1982	44
Large Eyed Night Bird	1982	45
Paradise False	1982	46
The Dragon	1982	47
Marking Time	1982	48

Prose & Petite Stories

...Skating Away...	2020	53
The Emperor's Wish	2009	56
The Clever Outdoorsman	2009	58
Late, but not Lost		
The Big Shiny Rock	2009	60
And the God Shaped Hole		

Beyond part three

Sweet Green Pea	1982	65
Papoose	1983	66
The Gypsy	1984	67
The Logic of Love and Flowers	1985	68
Vision of You	1987	69
Close Encounters of the Heavenly Kind	1991	70
Portholes	1991	71
Fast Cat & the Unrequited Love	1991	72
Opal Moon	1992	73
A Gypsy Prayer	1992	74
Drifting Rhyme	1993	75
Ants	1993	76

The Touch	1993	77
Sunday Best	1993	77
Love's Budding Elegy	1993	78
The Lost & Found	1993	80
When Two Gypsy Misfits Meet	1993	82
The Weight	1993	83
Wings of Eagles	1993	84
New Creatures	1994	85
Ride the Spirit	2007	86
Treasure Bay	2008	87
Joy of Mountains	2008	88
The Grabber	2009	90

Lyrics & Lullaby

Grandma's Little Prayer	2020	95
Way Down West	1980	96
High on Grace	2011	98
Old Man is Dead	2020	100
Playtime Is Over	2020	101

Beyond part four

A Stone's Throw	2009	105
Master Pillow	2009	106
Ode to the Lizard King	2009	108
The Dance	2010	110
Running Clouds	2010	111
Many a Shoes & Boots	2010	112
Quintiku	2010	113
Twin Sight	2010	113
Life So Strange	2010	114
Needles & Brick	2010	115
My Geisha	2010	116
Dog Dreams	2011	117

Sleepytime Rhymes & Prayers

Sleepytime Rhymes & Prayers   2008   123
The Reach   2011   124
Firefly   2011   124
Lord of All   2012   125
Sacred Stillness   2012   125
Elementary   2013   125

Beyond part five

No More Dust   2012   129
Sila Señorita   2012   130
The Whipping Post   2012   132
Life is Jungle   2013   134
Regret   2017   135
The Inside Linemen   2017   136
I Don't Chase the Butterfly   2017   137

An Beag Paidir n'Cosaint   2020   138
A Petite Prayer for Protection

Prayers of Night   2020   139~144
A Poet's Prayers

About the Author

Lawren DeLass is wordsmith and a thinker—a real word person in more ways than one. Not only is she now dedicated to the Words of the Good Book, but to the Word Himself and what He taught—the laws of cause and effect and the power that our words and thoughts have in effecting our lives, amongst other things. After all, the Creator spoke the universe into being by His Will and His Words.

The littérateur has cultivated and distilled the essence derived from her lifelong love affair with poetry writing down to a fine and fragrant, matured art form. Her navigations through the nether regions of the soul are profound due in part to a hard start in life having had a relatively brief, but intense psychotic mental illness. It is from this depth and the way she views the world around her that she is able to translate and project her vision to others.

At the end of the day, Lawren is an ordinary person who is unadorned with a long list of accolades, just the inveterate affinity for writing poetry as well as other creative pursuits. She is humbly decorated with an Associate Degree in Visual Communications aka graphic design which helped greatly in the creation of her life's representing work.

Prologue
A Brief, Poignant Retrospective

I was born in 1960 as the baby boom was winding down. I was raised loosely Catholic and in the public school system. I grew up in central/upstate New York and was one of a generation of children who endured, if you will—the first really big divorce boom. My parents who were married in the late fifties, pretty much fresh sprung out of high school, separated in the fall of 1969. I remember them riding off on dad's first Harley, a Sportster, heading out on what would be their last big excursion together. They were bound for the Woodstock music festival to celebrate his birthday which would be that Sunday, the seventeenth of August, amongst the fanfare of Rock's music greats of the time ...and Oh, how I wished I was going with them. Instead, my two younger brothers and I were left with the babysitter.

And so the journey began. Now separated, I was left with a disinterested and unaffectionate mother from as far back as I can remember—though she did what she could to help with the aftermath in the making. By age twelve and thirteen, with low self-esteem and lacking common-sense, I was distancing myself straight into the arms of the sixties and seventies Free Love generation's wave of hitch-hiking, partying, and Rock & Roll—and then on through the eighties ...whatever that was. Suffice it to say, that by this time, any communion I felt with religiosity was plummeting and already fully involved in a freefall out the window. When I was sixteen, I began hearing voices and unbeknownst to me, or anyone else for that matter, was developing a mental illness, a kind of fantasy world of my own. After being treated by a female, Hindu Indian, psychiatric intern named Doctor Gandhi for a few years, the most intense psychotic phase of the illness had succumbed. It didn't last too awfully long, and I was well into recovery by the time I was twenty. Living on assistance for a time, I then became a permanent member of the workforce at the age of twenty-four...

In 1992, at thirty-one, I became a Holy Spirit filled, Born-Again believer while living in a stretch of the Bible Belt, Nashville, Tennessee where I had moved in 1990. From here, there were many twists and turns and sundry hills and valleys, and I reckon there always will be to an extent. However, in 2017, the gospels and the whole Word of God was newly illuminated to me in a way I had never seen before. I believe, at long last, to have found Truth or *The* Truth, in a much deeper and more meaningful way. I have become a "Steward of the Mysteries," a term coined by the Apostle Paul, the writer of the majority of the New Testament. I am a "Disciple," which simply means disciplined. I have found the "Pearl of Great Price" and have bought the field. One thing is for sure —It's not about religion. There are no great, loud bells and whistles or grandiose displays that will announce we have arrived. This book is a journey and does not claim to be able to take the reader into the deeper, manifold facets of God, though I hope a few pearls of wisdom may be found. I can only nail up some signposts along the way. The narrow path you must pursue and navigate yourself.

Lawren DeLass

Note About the Creative Process

    I am not sentimental about leaving a poem the way it was originally written. I may come back to it several times, even years later, to make changes, polish, and improve it –letting it grow and express itself. Some may change and grow quite a lot, and others, hardly at all. While they always retain their original flavor and essence, there is a point that I feel a poem has reached its ultimate perfected state and will grow no more. Lately, with the more recent poems in the book, the works have arrived well-formed and nearly perfectly complete, line by line. The poems in this book are all aged to their full maturity. Therefore, the dates I have given are conception dates or birthdays, if you will –the years that they were conceived and born.

    • I have placed a small bullet in front of certain words in which I have taken advantage of my poetic license. If you find that a word has been misspelled, used improperly, or is not actually a word –it will likely have the afore mentioned symbol in front of it and will have been done purposefully.

Interior layout, illustrations, and literary work
By Lawren DeLass unless otherwise noted.

DEDICATED TO MY TEACHER AND COUNSELOR

B.D. Hyman

Simmering in the caldron for many a year,
Yet no witch's brew; Spun over, and over,
and over again, Infused with fragrant herbs
and savory spices, Some thistle and cat tail
and hogwort too; All steeped and steaming
in the iron pot with ladle and ready for you.

A Poem Written
In Childhood

Oh, Grandmother
Oh, Grandmother

Oh, Grandmother, Oh, Grandmother,
It's time for my breakfast,
pancakes and syrup
and tea that is brisk.

Oh, Grandmother, Oh, Grandmother,
It's time for my lunch
with soup and a sandwich
and crackers that crunch.

Oh, Grandmother, Oh, Grandmother,
It's time for my sup,
meat and potatoes
and milk in a cup.

Oh, Grandmother, Oh, Grandmother,
It's time for my bed
with a kiss and a hug
and prayers that are said.

Oh, Grandmother, Oh, Grandmother,
I love you so dear.
For you love me as well,
I never shall fear.

First Three Poems
Written as a Teenager

I Would Love
First Infatuation

When I first met you,
I was just a little girl,
an impressionable, sentimental,
and unaware little girl.

Your fetching face and form,
manifest royalty to me.
Intrigued by your wisdom,
your mysterious, strange ways
tangled me up inside and
I became your rapt captive.

Through my timid, virgin shell,
you aroused my senses.
As we kissed, I absorbed every
tender drop of your sensitivity.
A look, a touch, a feeling,
never known before until
that fine summer day at your door.

But wait awhile for it to grow
and I will make you see.
This twisted, thorny vine will loose
and flower's fragrance be.
I am ready for you now,
ready to know you,
ready for you to know me,
ready for your love.

Young Maiden's
<u>Folly of the Senses</u>
A Frolic in Innocence

Lie down in a meadow
of fresh wildflowers.
Sunny showers sprinkle on me
as I linger for hours.
My mind's high in heaven.
My spirit's set free.
I can feel nature's goodness
all around me.

Beneath a rainbow sky
till the sun dries the skin,
then mosey back the path
to where it begins.
How can I tell you
the joys I have seen?
Drink in the moist, white light,
crimsons and green.

Locked Up & Twisted

Infatuation Turns to Obsession / Innocence Lost
Written as ensuing psychosis loomed overhead

I saw him again,
this time like a dream,
a hazy, romantic, mysterious dream.
My mind filled with the fantasy and illusions
I loved from the past.
High on Maryjane,
I was locked up and twisted
with guilt and the smoke
that clouded about my head.

Then the people began to talk to me
as they had many times before.
From all around me come
the whispering voices in my mind.
When without a word uttered from my mouth,
you seemed to know me and spoke the truth,
professing aloud my thoughts as if in
possession of some magical gift.

What is it?
Does it show all over my face?
Am I dreaming?
Or do you read my mind?
Take me back to the love I once knew,
the thoughts so pure and beautiful,
the joys so at hand, poured out my soul,
that now only a mere taste I can feel
and does not nearly satisfy me enough.

Beyond

12

The Rose

Scarlet the ribbons
wound round and around,
then curling and flowing gracefully down.
Soft as satin to the touch,
no wonder you're admired so much.

Flourish green leaves deftly point to the east,
then to her blossoming west.
And sanguine the prick,
her armor of thorns
that protect her stately breast.

Her fragrance allure
to the strongest of men,
the jelly of bees for the Queen.
Given in adoration and in mourning,
God's lovely, royal display,
ever longing to be seen... the rose.

Ye Olde Love Poem

I love you at the point
love was born in your mind,
the climbing vines and buds
wrapping upward that
blossomed and spread
and now live in full bloom
vibrating gently within you with
a fragrance that seems to emanate
from every pore of your body.

Your body,
which has grown with the
smooth, round twists of masculine
curves like a tree in the forest,
trunk and branch features
that enchants me.

Your eyes,
like two cool pools of wisdom,
I know have seen the deepest
midnight hours, wrap me in velvet,
and to me your eyes alone,
the greatest gifts can deliver.

Riding the Wave

I feel a twinge of sorrow.
It comes on strong and scares me
like a dark wind that tries to blow
me down and under I go.
But I try my best to keep my balance,
knowing it to be much easier up here
riding the wave rather than swallowed
whole and drowning in its body.
Then the darkness passes.
I am safe for now.

Anyone will tell you, once you're under,
it's very painful being tossed about,
thrown around, and abused by the wave,
your head bobbing up only for the
occasional, momentary breath of fresh air.
It's difficult getting back up there.
You'll forget how it ever was to be riding.

So, when you get back up there
on that wave again, stay on top!
Keep riding that wave! In this life
we will know many a sorrow, but don't
let it swallow you alive!

Charcoals & Rust

Sometimes, when I look into the mirror,
I think of the rose I might have been.
I sometimes glimpse her,
   but only through a keyhole,
      seated at her vanity with a flower,
         soft and antique.

When I think of the rough
 and gypsy road I've taken,
  I see the tarnished rose I am,
   all the flowers I have missed,
      all the buds I might have kissed.

Now, the winter sky is dark with rage,
cold and black as the ace of spades.
I seek only the warm covers of my bed.
Swaddling in my cradle, I lament my
fading scars and treat my weary head.

But Oh, the valleys,
 those beautiful valleys,
  the shadows of dark and light,
   where in the darkness are lessons
      learned that lead us to what's right.

Bridges, canyons, rivers, plains,
 journeys of experience now rejected
  or embraced that fill an old trunk
   with memories and broken dreams,
      residues of the burning,
         residues of the flood...

... charcoals and rust
and the old china doll.

Over Yonder Hills

Over yonder hills
or in some valley,
there may be a child born.
With vines in her hands
and about her head,
I will set her on a lily pad.
I will carry her about
showing her all the world
and teach her many things.

When her eyes are filled with tears,
I will hum a song into her ears.
I shall peel the scales from her eyes,
so she may never wear that
unknowing clown's disguise.
Nor will she know the pain
and be leaving me to blame.

So, if by chance there ever
be a blind man in my midst,
I will speak to his eyes
till the scales fall off,
hence his blindness shall be fixed.
For children are most precious,
more precious than is gold.
And when the man can see again,
this truth he will behold.

Rain

Sprinkle dots my window,
speckles on the glass,
then soon the pane is a blur,
glazing like icing down a cake.

Suited now and walking,
the wet stuff on my face.
Large drops land in deep
like sparks fly up at knees
and double ringed circles
quick appear, then gone,
in shallows on the ground.

The mercurial liquid separates off
the road and flows into small rivers
that wind about the streets
like serpents –cool, steady slither.
When wind descends upon them,
it blows up ripples resembling scales.

In breeze stroked puddles,
I think I see long, streaming
aluminum icicles blowing in
the wind –rip, sparkle, and wave.

Downspouts gush anxiously,
bubbles mixed with foam,
and downpour sheets off
rooftops that don't collect...

... After the rain, the air is fresh
and clean, damp with renewed life.
With sun's return in a rainbow sky,
children play in ponds left behind
in the torrent's wake while the winding,
snake like streams rush into gullies
underground and disappear from sight.

Autumn's Inner Wind

Just around the corner is a cold, cold,
wind that makes me want to cry.
The name she claims is Autumn.
This year I'm greetin' her in style.
Gonna get me a taste of the highlife,
and Miller's ain't the kind I mean.
This swirling crown of colored
leaves gonna make me a queen.
In a long, black cloak and whirling with
the chilly breeze, dashing down the
gabled lanes, alabaster joie de vivre.

Her wistful song of dying, a joyous
symphony to me. Why in a season
known for death, I feel renewed and free?
Yes, she's come back to court me,
this time here to stay. No more chasin'
after them old dreams of yesterday.

Pinch of Country

The corn a row rides the roll
back into the far distant horizon
to greet the golden, rising sun.
Everything is clear and bright with
morning's indescribable light.

Patchwork quilt in shades
of Kelly and saffron, and forest
green trees embroider
the countryside scene.

At home in the crisp early air,
my mind and hands are busy to
market as I gather and prepare
farm fresh foods to fill our
stall at the buyer's fair.

My cup is creamed and full
with a grower's favored blend.
A bird's song is in my ear.
There's a spring in my step and
breath in my nostrils as I give
thanks to God for the harvest and
this wonderful bounty. Amen.

Dead Tomatoes

In a dry, dirt, neglected farmer's field,
bigger than a garden, yet smaller than a crop,
ridges of hard mud hump up in rows where
faded green plants lie withered and flat.

In the grooves of this wasted harvest sit soft,
overripe tomatoes baking in the hot summer
sun –missing the farmer's husky hands plucking
them from the vine, missing the kitchen,
missing the hands that so gently wash
them and prepares them for the sauce,
the sandwich, the salad.

Skin slips off the fragrant red mush as they
lay seeping back into the earth from which
they came –dying, wasted, sad, dead tomatoes.

Oh, Great Sheppard

Oh, Great Sheppard, we have wandered away.
Tell me why do so many go astray? Do the
sheep love the darkness more than the light,
losing their way by the lusts of their sight?
For the flesh is weak and so to their faith.
Search for them Savior for Your name's sake.

When will the black ones return to the fold?
When will their hearts to You only be sold?
For children are innocent, childhood pure.
But 'tis in the fruits of the Spirit that we endure.

Fantasy Ship

Tonight, the moon
lights up my iris garden
like a fantasy ship
on a softly twinkling starlit sea.
Green leaves a hissing.
A willow softly sways
as I joyously leap along cool grass,
pounding earth with my bare feet.

A mild breeze flows over me
when suddenly lightning illuminates
the black lit sky bright as day.
Summer heat lightning is all,
there'll be no rain tonight,
but 'tis a sign to end this play
of prance and dance
and muse myself inside.

Indiscreet

"Hey Mister... Yeah you, in the pinstriped suit
and gold pocket watch –can you give a poor girl
the time of day?" Gee whiz, man! Thanks a bunch.
Now, I'll be on my way. But before I go,
let me tell you what time it really is!

Do you have the time to give, to help your
neighbor and fellowman live?! And Hey,
Mister, can you spare a dime?"

It's time to WAKE UP! It's the twenty-first
century, no less! Time to live –not kill
and die! And though I may not know
you well, my friend, we are on this star together.

When clouds hover over you, does not
the light still shine inside? Or does the rain
drown the flame as if you were only a mere candle?
When the sky around your head is dark,
why must you stab my cloud of emotion
and make the rain fall for me?

Listen, and you will hear only the deep,
low sound of resounding silence –not the
battle cries of days gone by, for the only
battle worth fighting today, Mister,
is the battle for LOVE!

Old Spiritual Poems
By Various Authors

-❀- Are All the Children In? -❀-

Elizabeth Rosser

Are all the children in? The night is falling.
Storm clouds gather in the threatening west.
The lowing cattle seek a friendly shelter.
The bird flies to her nest.
The thunder crashes! Wilder grows the tempest!
And darkness settles o're the fearful din.
Oh, come shut the door and gather round
the hearthstone.
Are all the children in?

—◆—

Are all the children in? The night is falling,
when gilded sin doth walk about the streets.
At last, it biteth like a serpent!
Poisoned are the stolen sweets.
Mothers guard the feet of inexperience,
too prone to wander in the paths of sin.
Oh, shut the door of love against temptation!
Are all the children in?

—◆—

Are all the children in? The night is falling.
The dusk of death is hastening on a pace.
Hush now, children. The Lord is calling.
"Enter thou thy chamber and tarry there a space."
And when He comes, the King in all His glory,
Who died a shameful death our hearts to win,
Oh, may the gates of heaven shut round about us
with all His children in.

Conversion

Ophelia G. Adams

You ask me <u>how</u>
I gave my heart to Christ?
This, I do not know.
There came a yearning for Him
in my heart so long ago.
I found earth's flowers would fade and die
and wept for something that would satisfy.
And then, and then, somehow, I seemed to
dare, to lift my broken heart to Him in prayer.
This, I do not know. I cannot tell you *how*.
I only know He is my Savior now.

You ask me <u>when</u>
I gave my heart to Christ?
This, I cannot tell.
The day or just the hour,
I do not now remember well.
It must have been when I was alone,
the light of His forgiving Spirit shone
into my heart so clouded o'er with sin.
I think 'twas when, I trembling, let Him in.
This, I do not know. I cannot tell you *when*.
I only know He is so dear since then.

You ask me <u>where</u>
I gave my heart to Christ?
This, I cannot say.
That sacred place has faded
from my sight as yesterday.
Perhaps He thought it better...

... I should not remember where,
  how I should love that spot!
  I think I could not tear myself away,
  for I should wish forever there to stay.
  This, I do not know. I cannot tell you *where*.
  I only know He came and blessed me there.

  You ask me <u>why</u>
  I gave my heart to Christ?
  This, I can reply.
  It is a wondrous story.
  Listen, while I tell you why.
  My heart was drawn to seek His face.
  I was alone. I had no resting place.
  I heard of Him, how He had loved me,
  with a depth so great and height
  so far above all human ken.
  I longed for such a love to share.
  I sought it then with folded hands
  and upon my knees in prayer.

  You ask me <u>why</u>
  I thought this loving Christ
  would heed my humble prayer?
  I knew He died upon the cross for me.
  I am but one who nailed Him there.
  I heard His dying cry, "Father, forgive!"
  I saw Him drink death's cup that I might live.
  My head was bowed upon my breast in shame.
  He called me and in penitence I came.
  He heard my prayer! I cannot tell
  you *when,* nor *where,* nor *how.*
  I only know I love Him now.

The Ninety & Nine
(Dat Lil' Brack Sheep)
Ethel M. Colson

Po' lil' brack sheep what strayed away,
Done los' in de win' an' de rain,
An' de Shepherd He say, "O hirelin',
Go fin' My sheep again."
An' de hirelin' frown, "O Shepherd,
Dat sheep am brack an' bad."
But de Shepherd He smile, like dat lil' brack sheep
be de onlies' lamb He had.

An' He say, "O hirelin', hasten!
For de win' an' de rain am col',
An' dat lil' brack sheep be lonesome
Out dere, so far f'um de fol'.
An' de hirelin' frown, "O Shepherd,
Dat sheep is weak an' po'."
But de Shepherd He smile, like dat' lil' brack sheep
He luv it jes' all de mo'.

An' He say, "O hirelin', hasten!
For de frost am bitin' keen,
An' dat lil' brack sheep jes' shiv'rin'
In de storm an' de blas' between."
An' de hirelin' frown, "O Shepherd,
Dat sheep am a wuthless thing."
But de Shepherd He smile, like dat' lil' brack sheep
Be fine as a princely king.

An' He say, "O hirelin', hasten!
For de hail am beatin' hard,
An' dat lil' brack sheep git bruises...

... Way off f'um de sheepfol' yard."
An' de hirelin' frown, "O Shepherd,
Dat sheep is mos' worn out."
But de Shepherd He smile, like dat' lil' brack sheep
Jes' couldn't be done widout.

An' He say, "O hirelin', hasten!
For de winter is a'mos' here,
An' dat lil' brack sheep you shear it
'Till its po' skin is a'mos' clear."
An' de hirelin' frown, "O Shepherd,
Dat sheep is ol' an' gray."
But de Shepherd He smile, like dat' lil' brack sheep
Wuz fair as de break o' day.

An' He say, "O hirelin', hasten!
Lo, here is de ninety an' nine,
But dere way off f'um de sheepfol'
Is dat lil' brack sheep o' Mine!"
But de hirelin' frown, "O Shepherd,
De res' o' de sheep am here!"
But de Shepherd He smile, like dat' lil' brack sheep
He hol' it de mostes' dear.

An' de Shepherd go out in de darkness
W'ere de night wuz so col' an' bleak,
An' dat lil' brack sheep, He fin' it,
An' lay it agains' His cheek.
An' de hirelin' frown, "O Shepherd!"
Den he fell down on his knees.
But de Shepherd He smile, like the Lord He is,
Cuz dat lil' brack sheep am me!

Beyond
part two

A Yaqui Dream of Power

The Indian woman transformed herself
into a snake in a knee-deep stream
according to the Yaqui ways of knowledge.
Looking up through the water she sees
bright sky. Suddenly from above,
a dark shadow appears, coming down,
growing larger –a large, black bird to
seize her, to challenge her will,
her iron and her might.

The fight ensues in a tangled ball
of confusion. Splashing water and
feathers fly as they struggle for power
and ultimate control. When all at once
the two snarled creatures shot straight up
into the clear blue, blinded by the sun.

When the vision cleared,
the large bird, hanging by one wing,
was firmly gripped in the snake's jaws.
Then as if propelled by light, they
soared out of sight in a blur.

The Dawn of Eve

We arrive at dusk to the Paradise Resort.
At the front entrance we see a fiery,
lit fountain as we enter the palace like hotel
that will accommodate us. "Finally here,
high upon this pleasant, blue lake mountain.
We've dreamt of this retreat for such
a longtime." After check-in, we settle into our
Persian style villa for a good night's sleep.
In the morning we will explore
the back gardens.

Benches sit quietly in the grass and align
a curvaceous, white walkway beckoning
passersby to sit and seek a vision.
There for a time, we sit in the sun
gazing at the glazing fountains pushing
foamless upward, then slickly down
and about a menagerie of figurines.
Cool liquid runs off the back of a marble
Indian elephant with water from its
backward curling trunk.

Inhaling the pungent aroma of a nearby
cluster of hyacinths, a pale, golden pear
hangs in the mystic morning air as a young
snake slowly slithers through the grass
on the ground around the tree and
puts me in the mind of Eden...

...Later, we graze in a field of red poppies
gathering for a vase in our quarters.
It is now the dawn of eve. Let us
retire to the palace for the night.
On the agenda for tomorrow:
Ride the thoroughbred Arabians.
Run with dogs and chase butterflies.

The Queen's Dusky Jewels

In the moist, cool evening air, a peculiar light
paints the sky a deep, glowing, majestic hue of blue,
descending with the day down the horizon line
now washing the rolling field a brilliant, sun born pink
where six knights on horseback ride for the Queen.
She has requested their services in retrieving
some pilfered jewels and they are now
returning with the goods.

Oh, how pleased she will be to once again see her
beloved brooch, her ring, her pearls, and more.

After the delivery, the knights will feast and dine
with turkey on the drumstick and spirits of beer
and wine. Frisky wenches entertain,
but one knight looks off afar.
He's making designs on the
widowed queen, a plan
to steal her heart.

Pink Poppies

I sat beneath a willow,
beside a palace pond.
Gazing beyond the eyes
of a fanned peacock, I could
see fields of hazy pink and mauve
poppies owned by an Opium Queen.

There in the palace and
lounging on the pillows,
puffing her hookah,
the Queen was far too high
and self-absorbed to keep
proper watch over her
blossoming daughter.

One day as she ran and played,
she could not hear her mother's call.
Caught in the cool, descending evening
shade, she was captured by the night.

So, once again and like clockwork,
the night sat down to stare into his
massive, murky mirror. There he saw
as most would slumber, many macabre
things and the odious faces of those who
would use the cover of night to do their
evil deeds that would blind the princess
with fear, if only she could see...

... Sent away was her hero
and cast off of her throne,
she was thrown into a dungeon
where she braved the dark alone.
Clouded over were her eyes
by the thick, black ink. There she
was bound for many moons.

Once, at last, released,
she made the acquaintance
of many a fine prince who
one by one did lie with her
beside a single candle's light
inside the blanket of the night.

From within the shroud she grew,
having fantastic dreams and visions
as elusive as she and her happiness.

Then, late one evening and taken aback,
the shadows of darkness ran darker.
The night, did he, wax bolder –dancing
harder, blacker, colder. When from
out of nowhere came a red, hot fire as
if from the mouth of a dragon, nearly
tangible, to lick her smoldering spirit...

... "What was that?" she asked,
and felt not well.
"Could this be a flame from hell?"

Something evil mounted higher
to ride her soul to destruction.

Until one day, returned the Prince
of the peacock, the true Emperor of
the field, the one who is King of kings
and Lord of all lords. Her Heavenly
Father stepped in to save and softly
summoned the love she freely gave.

Now, once again, in the light,
no longer hounded by the night.
Like a child she laughs and plays
in yonder fields all her days.

The City is Dying

In foggy old London town, the clouds hang low.
The city I come from is generally gray.
Known for its overcast skies, a sheet
of cloud lingers two thirds of the year.

Overcast, gloomy days in the city are
not like those in the country. In the
country we accept it as organic and
the ways of nature. Death and rebirth
have their cycles. But here in the
concrete jungle, things only erode,
crack and crumble, and we subconsciously
blame the city for the weather.
"Gray city, gray day –DAMN gloomy city!"
Even the church bell's ring sounds gray today.
·Monstorious buildings on all sides crowds even
the mind. Crowds of people crowd the body.

In the country the bird of peace can fly low and
come to rest on our rooftops. Someday, I will
make my home in the country. My soul will
flourish there. For here in the city there
is little grass, nor the room to grow.

The Zoo Lion

At an old-time zoo built in the second
decade of the 1900s, I was a child
in the 1960s. Small shoes crunch over peanut
shells and popcorn as I read a sign that says:
    DON'T FEED THE ANIMALS

Iron barred cages align the one isle prison.
Cobblestone leads tiny feet to a small,
bogus rock pond in the corner, home
to some turtles, lizards, and fish.

A dark, murky aquarium contains
a twisted bundle of snakes.
Animal odors rise to the occasion
when I see some monkeys, baboons,
and an anxiously pacing tiger.

And then there is the lion, the majestic lion.
Sympathetic on lookers peer in at the poor
beast lying there growing flabby and weak
in its primary prison of flesh, and I think...
Is this the King of Beasts?

All in a moment's contemplation,
I devised a plan to return after dark
when no one is around and release the regal
creature to roam free and live out the rest
of its days in liberty. With a tear in my
eye and popcorn in my mouth, we slowly
move on to the next cage.

Little Big Head

Lying on a soft carpet of cool, green grass, one day
when I was a child, I felt like a feather floating
on the summer breeze with eyes that could see the
crystal clear, blue sky, and ears that could hear the
whispering of nearby wild fields and the
hissing of the leaves in trees.

Was it a real day or just a dream?
inside a crystal ball, or maybe just a bubble?
It was all in a moment that lingered… when we pull
on the strings of memory that hang in our minds.

At story's end, the vision floated away in a pink
balloon, far, faraway up into the cloudless blue,
becoming a tiny speck in my eye as it disappeared
from sight a long, long time ago.

Lost Little Babe

The lost little babe took a dip in a stream,
and being swept away she arrived at a beam.
When there she stood up to gaze
and implored in a curious tone,
"Where does this beam come from?
Where does this ray lead?
There's only one way to find out.
I'll climb it and see!"

When then she climbed
but a fraction of the way,
she felt a burning heat intensify.
Glaring light shown in her childish face,
casting pain into her eyes.
"This star's too bright and shiny for me.
It flares too hot and strong."

Then a thunderous, booming voice
blew her of the beam saying,

"GET BACK WHERE YOU BELONG!"

Large Eyed Night Bird

I made it to the other side, swam
the stormy sea. I feel like a mirror
and it's lookin' at me. I've always
been right, never been wrong.
Life's been a picnic all along.

I am leaving this place tonight,
swimming out the unknown sea.
Where the birds can swim and
the fish can fly, the lines are
drawn by the all-seeing eye.

The brush is in my hand. There are
colors for the taking. Another universe
is in the making. Swirling hues splash the
sides with green; moonlit leaves cascade,
the branches of a fabled tree where a
large eyed night bird is staring at me.

WHoo might you be?
WHoo might you be?

Paradise False

There is no true glamour, no real class,
not so long as the earth and its inhabitants
continue to suffer. Glamour is the illusion,
a tool or projection used by the evil one.
Opulence is an image of paradise false.
This is No paradise! –No Shangri-La!
We are living in a cursed world!

The fading beauty paints her face
with brushes and assorted pigments,
a fresh new canvas to put on the
day with a sultry smile. And Oh,
what a difference a little line doth make.
Standing statuesque, gilded and glowing,
translucent, sheer, and frosted as a
butterfly's wing. Under the spell of the
bright, hot lights, all that glitters seems
as gold. Then the oils begin to run.

Elegance is to partake of beauty,
the enjoyment of finer things, something
to be grateful for and hope to share
like drinking select, aged wine from a
crystal, stemmed glass, or a cold, frosty
mug of beer and good food with companions
and kin. But let us not be frivolous
and wasteful, my friends, or apathetic
to humanity's plight, nor to the hygiene
of this fierce and lovely lady we call earth...

...What is vogue, but a painted lady?
   What is allure, but a smoky screen?
      – A practice in vanity?

Beneath a veil of deception, lies,
the wearer of the mask.
Live, laugh, love, give –though try as we may,
try as we might, we will never reach
nirvana here, in this paradise false.

The Dragon

The newborn dragon slashes and claws blindly
through the mystic, morning air of our minds,
propelled by an intense, fiery hunger
and relentless, subconscious force,
driven by passion and the need to create.
Somewhere in the secret depths of our
imagination, it frolics and follies.

Sometimes we catch a glimpse of it laughing
and rolling around in the pit of our bellies,
until one day it is awakened, but only
in the dreams of the surrogate. In a selfish,
joyous, frenzy to be alive, it carelessly flashes
its golden eyes and fury about, flailing its
awful limbs, snorting with its hot breath,
and whipping its powerful, violent tail.

Watch Out!

Marking Time

One week passes, then another
without fail, little desire for
material things, no desire to change.

Do the wash. Hang it out on the line,
enough colored bandanas to wear
for two weeks, six different ways,
drying in the sun and waving like
freak flags blowing high in the wind,
all worn with denim blues and
a simple, black cotton tee like
Jerry Garcia playing to his
dancing tie-dyed kids.

Take yourself out to dinner.
My choice tonight —*thee* best,
authentic, Italian pizza.
Get a friend on the horn.
Walkout into night, looking
for a lost and lamenting scene.
Drink a few brews. Pour a little wine.
Check please! Thank you, feeling fine!

Here at the mill, we run the machines
of the dirty, daily grind like a needle
in a tight groove, a regular routine.
I watch my savings grow at a slow,
but steady pace, saving for a move
to another place far, faraway
from the likes of here.

50

Prose & Petite Stories

A Wonderful Day Skating Away Upriver in Black & White

Our house was a gingerbread Victorian that sat high on a bank of the Shawshine River in New England. One day in mid-February came a warm rain that melted most of the snow but left the frozen solid river a smooth and gleaming sheet of magnificent ice. I made plans to skate the very next day. I was fifteen, that year in 1927. When I rose that Saturday, it was about 10:30. I washed, poured myself a glass of juice, and made two slices of French toast in the iron griddle and spread them with jam. I put on my two-piece long johns and two pairs of socks. I bought my skates a size larger to accommodate the extra warm stockings. I dressed and went out to the back porch that overlooks the river and sat on the wooden bench to lace up my skates. I made my way out to the top of the railroad tie steps that led down to the river wearing a gray sweater under a belted, Navy style pea coat, black beret, and matching wool leggings along with my white skates.

I launched off the ice crusted, small pebble beach where we would swim in the summer and onto the crystal, satin ice with a shoulder bag across my chest containing a bologna and cheese on rye, a cold drink, and two oatmeal raisin cookies mom had made the night before. By this time, it was nearing noon. It was not a sunny day, but not a gloomy one either. Everything seemed bright. As I skated away on the river, I felt so free and alive like I was flying. Gliding and drifting along and taking the occasion to curve my lines and spin; extend my leg out behind me, and skate backwards in a wavy motion, I was filled with...

a sense of pure joy and inspiration. I passed under the brewery's straight, iron bridge and around a tree lined bend where I happened on a man practicing his figure skating. He was quite good! We waved and said hello as I passed. It seemed I could skate forever and become neither cold nor tired. In fact, I was already much further upriver than I had ever skated before, but I was not worried. I was loving every minute of my midday, February excursion. Next, I came upon some children playing in an alcove of ice. A boy and two girls were having the grandest time laughing while slipping and sliding in their boots. As they were chortling and falling all over each other, I could hear them repeating the words, "good, old-fashioned fun."

Finally, but nowhere near weary, I met a group of town's people from the next town up who were also skating. They had made a fire and were sharing hot cocoa. Well into the day, I took the opportunity to have some, eat my lunch, and warm by the fire. Their cheeks were rosy, and their eyes were as bright and glowing as the ice. Someone snapped a picture. Courtland people are very nice.

As I set out back home, I knew I had already skated about eight miles. My heart was still soaring and gleeful. The sky was just beginning to dim ever so slightly. I was surprised that neither coldness nor fatigue had yet set in. I must have bundled well. The skies then really became a sight to see. These winter skies were the most beautiful I've ever seen —swashes of thick, windswept clouds smooth as custard, set in the haze with peeks of clearing that were glowing aqua. Their soft blue-gray underbellies were painted in a variety of slightly muted pastel colors, yet still lit by the setting sun. Every color was present. I was checking to see if they were all there: lavender, green, yellow, orange, blue ...and of course, pink. The softness of the clouds, the light, and the assortment of colors was breathtaking and unlike anything I'd ever seen before or since. It was a rare sight indeed.

Part of the way back, I passed five teenage boys taking advantage of the remaining daylight to play a game of hockey. Further down, a red fox peered at me from the brushes on...

the bank. Now, back in familiar territory, a young man, bent over and holding his hands behind his back, nodded and speed skated past me around a bend and out of sight. Crows cawed in the trees and hawks flew overhead. From a distance, a group of black figures climb and ride their sleds downhill where the snow didn't melt. The awesome clouds were now all but gone. And, lo and behold, as the sun sank all the more into the horizon line, so did I feel the first vestiges of the cold soaking into my flesh. Only a mile or so from home, the sun had gone down be-hind the hills. The moon was painting the darkness a soft, radiant gray. Its bright reflections were glistening on the ice.

Home now, onto the icy pebbled beach and up the railroad tie steps, my blades seemed to dig into the wood. On the bench, I removed my skates. When I stepped inside, the grandfather clock read 5:30. Mother was making dinner and asked me what I'd been up to. I told her only part of the wondrous story. "I will make you some tea," she said as I wound up in the heavy afghan blanket on the couch in front of the fire. There warming up, I began to ruminate over this most glorious escapade that shall be amongst my fondest memories for a very longtime to come.

The Emperor's Wish

Long ago there was a thoughtful Chinese Emperor who wished to devise a new method of marking time. While intently pondering the subject, in a moment of sheer inspiration, he happened upon an idea. He would gather all the animals of the kingdom riverside, just outside the palace courtyard, to take part in a race. And that is precisely what he did. He spoke to the assembled creatures of various sort and size and challenged them. "The first twelve of you to make it across the river will be the chosen few to mark time; one year to each of you, and in the order you make it to the other side, first to last," commissioned the Emperor. The animals were over the moon! They were overjoyed at the chance to compete for the awesome privilege of representing a year and marking time.

Before the competition was to commence at the Emperor's dropping of a feather, the cat and the rat who were great companions were worried and contemplating what to do for they were weak and slow swimmers. Suddenly, the rat came up with a plan. He entreated the kindhearted, muscular ox to let them ride his back. "Sure, why not," succumbed the ox. When the Emperor released the feather from his balcony and it finally alighted onto the ground, they all jumped into the deep waters of the river with a big splash.

There were at least fifty kinds of animals, all swimming as fast and as hard as they could. Nevertheless, the massive ox promptly took the lead with the cat and the rat hanging on tight to its broad back. The pig and sheep paddled like the dog; the snake squiggled; the rooster flapped; the horse swished and...

strode; the rabbit hopped and flopped, and the monkey kick-ed and flailed at the hopeful waters of the river's surface. When halfway across, the cat and the rat were very pleased with their position, for the ox, with his strong powerful legs was still holding first place. Fast approaching the banks of the river, the gritty rat, having hardly even a thought, and without warning, pushed the cat off the ox's back and into the river where it clawed the water and struggled frantically.

Closer and closer to land they drew, the rat still holding fast the back of the ox. Only a few feet from the edge, the rat once again acted with fierce and unwavering determination. He hopped up onto the ox's head; then, with all its might —leapt onto the slippery mud and grass of the river's bank! Rats are not fast swimmers, but they are good jumpers. So, the Emperor honored the clever rat by naming the first year after him. The New Year was to begin the very next day, the first ever, "Year of the Rat."

Needless to say, the good-natured ox was a bit dis-mayed. But there were no rules in this race, only that they make it to the other side and do it fast! Just the same, the ox was awarded the second year to be his namesake, "The Year of the Ox." And so, on it went: the rat, the ox, the tiger, the rabbit, the dragon, the snake, the horse, the sheep, the monkey, the rooster, the dog, and the pig—they were all winners that day! The poor cat didn't even place. Sadly though, that day a great friendship was lost. For from that day forward the cat and the rat who had been the best of friends, became mortal enemies, and all the cat's descendants have chased and eaten all the rats descendants ever since.

The Clever Outdoorsman
Late, but not Lost By Jack & Lawren DeLass

In the fall of 1962, during a time when deer were scarce in the Adirondack Mountains, Norval was winding down a full month of hunting. It was midafternoon when from 300 yards away on the opposite side of the marsh; he spotted an eight-point buck. It was the same buck his twenty-four-year-old son, Jack, had shot at the day before with his Winchester 30/30. He thought he'd shot it, but they discovered he'd missed when the buck rose up off the ice it had slipped on in its fright and ran off. Jack packed up and left the hunt that evening to return to work. Now, with the buck in Norval's sights, he aimed high and shot, but the bullet wound up going under the buck. The buck never moved because the shot came from so far away it didn't hear it. With the .348 Winchester elephant gun, aiming even higher, he shot again. This time the bullet went over the buck. With the third shot, the buck went down.

It was two o'clock and Norval was at the northeast side of the marsh when he started to drag the buck out of the woods. Knowing the distance he had to travel, he realized he'd never make it out before dark at the speed he was going. Having seen bear tracks earlier, he also knew he could not leave the kill there overnight or he'd have nothing but bloody pieces to return to the next day, so he started heading towards an old, abandoned logging camp. There, with the sun going down fast upon him, he took off his one-piece long johns and dressed the deer. Norval hoped the deer would look human or at least like something other than animal to the bear. He then laid the buck...

atop a big woodpile and urinated around the lumber to repel the bear with his human scent. He had to wait there until the moon was bright and high in the sky to see well enough to make his way. Norval then proceeded to walk out of the woods alone.

In the meantime, the owner of the Deerhead Inn sent out a search party looking for him. This rustic tavern is where, during hunting season, acquisitions of deer hung from the edges of the roof in the crisp, cold Adirondack air. Father and son would drink a few beers there before retiring to their campsite and tent for the night. Norval heard shots and people yelling, but he had no idea they were looking for him. Because, you see...my grandfather always knew exactly where he was at all times. He was an expert outdoorsman: fishing, canoeing, snowshoeing, you name it. Norval was a man of the Finger Lakes and the northern tier. He was also a racecar driver, a builder, and an inventor. Eventually, he met up with a member of the rescue party and asked, "What's going on?" "We're looking for you!" replied the searcher. "Why? I'm not lost!" The next morning, he went back to claim his prize and found frustrated bear tracks all around the woodpile. Norval kept the eight-point rack as a trophy and a fond memory. It is now in his son Jack's proud possession. But can you imagine the sight, if you happened onto this —a deer decked out in full, gray union suit?!

The Big, Shiny Rock
& the God Shaped Hole

When a young person, or anyone for that matter, feels a sense of barrenness and void in their soul, the tendency is to stuff it with anything they think might make them feel better. What they really need is to seek answers in something bigger than themselves. Knowledge and the love of the Creator can guide them on their way and help them to make wise decisions.

✧ For the youthful, those who lack wisdom and experience, the allure of the enigmatic—the unknowns of their lives—sparkle and shine like huge diamond. It rotates around slowly, casting brilliant rays from its facets into their eyes, giving them the hope and promise of satisfying some empty place inside. The God shaped hole that exists in all of us can be filled with all sorts of things. Sex, intoxicants, exhibition, popular idols, glamour, and various other interests and intrigues take care of some of it. All these things artificially and temporarily quell the need for love, attention, the "feel good," and adoration. Respectively though, one should be wary and take heed. Too much experimentation can lead to feelings of guilt and shame. It can be a tenuous balance.

✧ The love we first experience comes from the outside like a shining sun and nourishing rain from above; then, grows like a flower within. When children continue to be fed and nurtured with enough of the real stuff, along with a lot of good information and practical knowledge, like a fertilizer encouraging...

wisdom—the diamond won't seem so bright and shiny. They will carry it around in their pockets like a jewel encrusted compass feeling confident they already possess the goods—the answers to the mysteries others have their sights set on and are so hungry and anxious to explore, and it will help them avoid the miry pitfalls suffered by other more foolish navigators.

You, the Father, Son, & the Holy Spirit, a Winning Team!

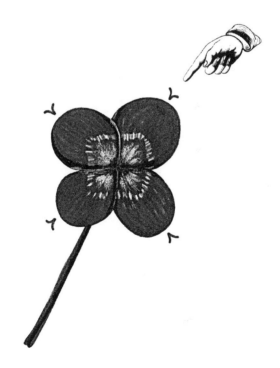

Beyond
part three

Sweet Green Pea

Once, a grave mistake was made that caused
a gift to be waylaid. Smug in the month of August,
turned sweet and twenty-two, dark in summer
breezes on youthful skin, she lay reclined, her gift
delayed until revealed another day.

The singer and the queen compete in dire madness,
always one step ahead and two steps behind
the other. Darkly made-up eyes glisten and glare.
Whirling gowns swiftly shift and swirl, and they dance,
and they dance, like two tightly spinning tops.
Unwittingly they connect, begin to wobble and lose
control until finally, they spill over. Wiped out,
white noggins crash and collide, their dresses
splayed out on the floor.

Once set to receive the divine gift of an inspired race,
no longer to be postponed, from out of the sky on
a saucer will arrive a sweet green pea, which will set
the trends for the twenty-first century.

Who will be next, the next to receive?
Who will be the next one of you to be set free?
Why, it's a newly awakened sybarite, still sleepy
eyed but ready to roll, just another ·felion
on the prowl, roaming in the tall grass,
lurkin' in the brilliant, dark spaces of life.

<u>Papoose</u>

A young native woman squats, leaning against a tree.
Her dark skin glistens with sweat as she writhes
in pain. The Indian babe falls out onto the grass under
the tree and squints at the mid-morning sun splintering
through the branches.

She picks up the bloody boy and cries with relief
and joy –a raksa'a born to a first time gnoha. She cuts
the cord with her knife and washes him with water she
brought in a treated hide, then wraps him in ·softskins
and places him to her breast.

Now, walking with the bundle, she feels
a strange, surreal excitement in the pit of her belly.
At home the new mother is greeted by her
happy clan and receives a warm, proud embrace
from her Iroquois man.

A type of framed carrier called a cradle board
has been made and is leaning against the lodge.
Secured upright anywhere with baby inside;
upon gnoha's shoulders; hung in the dwelling
or on a tree or a post, will make it easier for her to
do her daily tasks. The infant may also be tied-up
in blanket sling and carried on her back.

Other women of the tribe bring the gnoha extra ·softskins,
tiny clothes, and moccasins they made for the little
newcomer. For a time, she and the newborn will rest in
the longhouse awaiting a dream or a vision sent down from
sky world by the Great Spirit to be the child's name.

The Gypsy

The gypsy's dress a whirl was torn but sewn again.
Red as blood were her two lips. And as
her dress, her heart was torn
amid two loves betwixt.

The garb of her tradition, black vest and ribbons red,
dowry coin hangs from laces black
and scarves about her head.

The gypsy woman dances wildly encircling the fire.
Sparks fly up at raven hair.
Men clap and feel desire.

Frisky fiddles sound through the crisp night air
and so too the jingle of her
tambourine bells ring.

Sometimes sad and mournful, frisky fiddles wane.
In the day God sends His reckoning
a gypsy soul feels pain.

Free and stirring was her spirit and the caravan was
life's way, from city to village, and town
to town, life lived from day to day.

Eyes aglow with passion, deep and black as coal,
warmed at night by campfire's light, the flames,
the men, and song, that bind
the band of many, sojourning
fills a life that's long.

The Logic of Love & Flowers

Disillusioned again, gazing into the fervent fire,
I thought I saw love's eyes reflecting in the flames.
Now, all love seems a cruel and superficial game
based on looks, size, and the fatness of your purse.
Spurned again in the usual passionate play,
exact your ounce of flesh from my heart.

Now, my hope lingers inside the pedals
of a delicate flower, a seed or bulb that when
planted and nurtured –nutrients, sun, and a little rain,
becomes a beautiful, aromatic thing, made by God,
beloved by all, pleasing to the nose and eye.
If God designed a marvel such as this, maybe there
is hope! Did He also create a hidden strand,
one that binds a woman and a man? 'Tis said that
once entwined together by God, with God,
we form a braid stronger than any woven cord.

The bee in search of fine, sweet nectar,
carries a potent powder from one blossom
to the next and a miracle of creation takes place.
This tiny, winged creature is a type of god to the
flower, the main player in its procreation.
Yes, we may connect. Yet, we all stand alone,
our faces shining to the sun. Though do remember
to always think twice! Don't answer only to the buzz,
the bells and whistles of the celebration,
lest ye might ·bee stung...

...So, if the flower's seed be real, why not if guarded
and cherished, cannot love also be real?
Perhaps the lovely, fragrant flower knows the truth.

Vision of You

The eyes of my mind have seen you.
From within and without,
you are a work of art,
like an iridescent vase
that holds precious things,
polished stones, deep mysteries,
and the fragrance of jasmine.

Strokes of darkness,
strokes of light,
expressive hues incite delight.

Deep within you
is a brilliant, shining egg
arrayed and glorious glowing.
When the delicate, frosty shell
is finally cracked, the contents
will be revealed as it flows out its
glistening, golden center,
in my vision of you.

Close Encounters of the Heavenly Kind

The hounds of hell are tracking me.
I've been running many a night.
They want to collect their pound of flesh
for I've been courting the dark angel.
I am like a moth caught in your twisted web.
You charmed me using God's good gifts.
Spoiled and defiled, I swim in the depths
of your shadowy bog.

But the Lord of all has other plans and
wakens me just before dawn with the
blissful news. I feel Your presence beside me.
Your light envelopes me in the dark.
Your Holy Spirit collides with mine
and the contrast is woefully stark.
I am stricken with awe and an unspeakably
deep sense of peace that surpasses
understanding –an absolute, indescribable,
warm love and a sure knowledge You are real.

I beg and babble in Your awesome attendance:
"I know You're real! I feel it in my spirit.
I can feel You at the very core of my being!
I love You Lord. I truly do, so very much.
I always have! Please don't forget that.
Please don't forget me!"

After the encounter, I gently drift back
to sleep. Soon, the memory fades into
the hustle and bustle of daily affairs.
Yet, this experience won't be forgotten...

... for it is among the very seeds of my salvation.
  Yes, I was touched! I know I was.
  He touched me down deep in my soul!
  This is my revelation in the night,
  the dark night You opened the door
  and showed Yourself to me.

Portholes

Some people move slow and deep like submarines
peering out their portholes, experiencing the world at
a drift's speed with wide eyed wonder at every turn.

Others merge more quickly like race cars, speeding
down every scenic route and miss everything,
bypassing all the beauty as the world outside
their window flies by in fast motion, just a blur.

Don't forget to stop
& smell the roses.

Fast Cat & the Unrequited Love

How can I make you see the things I see in me?
  How can I make you see the things I see in you?
  How can I make you remember me?

So many beautiful scenes I see, in you, in me,
  and so many ·unscenes, things I didn't
    want to see but did.
      Yet, it's all here just the same flickering inside.

We had our moments burnin' hot at the wick,
  runnin' down the candle stick. You started a fire
    in me that's now been doused, snuffed out between
a thumb and fingertip, left only to smolder
  and slowly die in a wisp of smoke.
      Yet, it's all here just the same flickering inside.

Moves I made and wanted to make
  and moves I didn't want to make but had to.
    I see so many wonderful things in you
that I wonder ...could you ever see in me? Maybe you
  did and you're just not saying. But as you well know,
      at any given moment you can think of me
        down this corridor of time.
          I'm still here. You're still there.
            There's still a flame just the same
              flickering inside, deep within the soul.

Opal Moon

God's people shall rejoice, praise His holy name.
I am God's people, one of His, a jasper child.

I love the places You've shown me Lord, the pure
palace of the crystal heart. Here the opal moon
shines so bright it almost hurts my eyes. We should
be like that moon, reflecting the Son's magnificent light.

How in the world can a dead man rise? How will he
ever shine? How can he know Your love? Awaken,
Oh, spirit man! Rise and receive the living waters.
Let your dry bones dance and be replenished.

Yes, our souls should dance. Yes, our souls
should sing. Gratefulness to our Creator these living
stones bring! With a desire to give and wish to grow,
Lord, make me what You want me to be
under the opal moon.

A Gypsy Prayer

Lord, what shall I do, keep on
traveling, movin' down the road,
follow the gypsy plan?
Looking for love, not dying,
missing, remembering,
but never crying. –Ya live,
ya love, ya learn, and then ya leave.

Lawren DeLass

Lord, I love my wandering, exploring new
places and new things, the cultures of people
and the way they live. –Not one house, not one land,
not one city, not one man. Someday, I'll go back
to see the ones I love, maybe even see you again,
but for now I'm just riding the big wheel killin' time,
waiting for my young men to grow older,
come time to settle down.

Love could probably stop my drifting. Papa didn't
raise no fool. Or perhaps another wayward stranger
will join me on a leg or two. –Wheels keep on turning,
souls endlessly yearning. The rhythm of the road
gets in your soul, tied up with scarves like a
gypsy hobo. Somewhere there's an end for me,
but I've no idea when or where it might be. Dear God,
grant me the time for learning. Let my creative
energy flow. And let me live to find out. Amen.

Drifting Rhyme

Where do you see yourself when you
leave this world and go on to the next?
Can you put yourself where you want to be?
Do you think you have the power?
Or do we need a helping hand,
a teacher, guide, a guru, someone,
to take us up to higher ground?
Jesus is my guru, Most High Priest.

So, are you in a Persian palace
on a magic carpet ride,
lounging on a cloud
in a self-made paradise?

Maybe dancing on a moonbeam,
colors swirling all around,
with all your friends in hell
hot partying down?
Are you kneeling at the throne
of a queen unseen?!

Tell me all you servants,
do you really know the King,
or are you only drifting,
scattered on an unknown sea?

Ants

Can you even begin to imagine how great God is?
How small we are, from His place on high compared
to the Almighty, like ants or a grain in a vast sea of
sand –a tiny spark that flies and quickly dies.

All righteous, all holy, all just, all merciful,
Father of Creation. Our most powerful, victorious
moment –Not some superman's cape, but filthy
rags, if not in connection with Him.

Topping steeples across the world where ravens perch
like harbingers of doom waiting to snatch fallen fruit,
the drama and the symbolism of the cross alerts us to
a higher call. Though many will perish due to a lack
of knowledge and failure to answer.

Songs of the passion play. We awaken to a new day.
Rolling the stone, He rises, Oh, my Soul! Bright and
shinning like a matchless sun. I take His hand
and start to walk before I can learn to run.

The Touch

After hearing the songs of love, the Holy
Spirit came down and taken under His wing,
He tarried with me through the streets of the city.
There along the boulevard, I began to discern
genuine good from evil, His presence protecting
and guiding my movements, feeling a clean warmth
in my heart like a mighty friend who's near, at my side.

At the big tent revival, my eyes were alight
with the reception of truth and they told me,
"God's Word shall not return unto Him void."
But the Spirit leaving seed, falling on dry,
rocky ground, after some days departed.
With a mournful cry and ascending like a dove,
the Spirit sailed back up into Heaven carrying
a note for the Father of a soul softening moment
of victory and coming deliverance tale to tell...

Sunday Best

My babies are dressed in their Sunday Best.
They're anxious to come out and play.
Bowties, dresses, and patent leather shoes,
they want to be seen, to sing you a tune.
They want to get down in the dirt.
But I won't let them... No Siree
–till service is over and they've put on
their overalls and pantaloons.

Love's Budding Elegy

God forbid I should ever want again.
My handsome flower plucked away by
a common woman. A beautiful dream
lost to someone more typical, more vanilla.

Kicked off the merry-go-round once again,
one final plunge of the knife and here I am.
I, the all ·aloner –obscure, opaque, enigma,
and sometimes subtle pariah, marching to
the only beat I know, a square peg in a sea
of round holes. Where do I fit?

Given a strong mind, I believe God made me
to think, to use what He gave me, to write
and create. So, let me sing my song, but let
me sing it in a daylight place, not some dark
lion's den. Or let me be a light in the darkness.

I am hurt and feel like a misfit again.
But Oh, how I run to You Lord and
remember the days I didn't know You,
all alone, with no shelter from the storm.

But the storm rages on just outside Your love,
raging like a blue-gray sensual sea where I use
to be tossed about. I can still feel the waves
slapping me and crashing the shore.

I get mad. A tear wells to my eye. Why can't
I be more like You Jesus, love more all the time?!
And will another be my lover?! I like a man who...

... knows the blues but loves You too.
  With a heart full of forgiveness and more,
  I am still here waiting for my slice of the pie.

  So, can I dance for You Lord?! Can I ride
  the wild, multicolored tide for just a little while?!
  With Your hand leading me, I can do anything
                    −and I can sing!

        HALLEL −U −JAH! ...HALLEL −U −JAH!
        ... PRAI −SES ...TO ...THE ...KING!

A rendition of a crayon
drawing done as a child

The Lost & Found

All alone in the dark, Satan's accusatory
finger is pointed squarely at me, and it hurts.
Blamed for things I've done.
Blamed for things I haven't done.
I'm beginning to think I did do the crime.

The Savior knocks at the door, but it sounds like
miles away. Someone out there must know the
truth —Someone! God knows I didn't do it —God knows!
He was there as my only ally, though not near.

I am lying here in the devil's playground, land of knives
and gunfire, baseball bats, my cleated and spiked
mashing boots, and walking the razor's edge barefoot.

Frequent attacks by ten-thousand maniacs,
Hannibal cannibals, Sunday morning front stoop killers,
BTK devourers and other sex crazed imps, all sneaking
up from behind when not guarding your ass. It's your
own personal bloodbath compliments of Satan
the motel manager. He will be your tour guide
through this labyrinth of horrors...

... From his control room, onto the television sets and the other screens of our lives, he pipes in scenes of seductiveness, violence, and pornography, designed to overheat and pollute the mind and body.

Perversions and thoughts more twisted than spiral macaroni, pleasure and pain all the way, then complete confusion. What do you reach for? What saves you but a crack at self-righteous wit that gives you enough courage to snap back? Tiny lashes feel like feathers to the amused beast.

Lost boy, chameleon prince, reaching for an unknown's hand in strange and new, bewildering land screams, "Jesus, Save Us!" Desolation and bondage, sensual pleasures that lead nowhere, seeking to pack an aching wound.

–"I need a drug, she cried! Shoot me up! I need a fix –something to make me feel good again!" If I could just run out naked in the rain I might be alright. Jesus, I need a friend.

When Two Gypsy Misfits Meet

Walking peaceful streets
in the hours after midnight,
under a streetlights glow,
between a city and a suburb,
enjoying the warm, summer night air,
watching my shadow's long
hair blowing in the wind.
Past a park, through the dark,
down the street I move.

Reaching for a feeling of my own
creation and illusions almost tangible.
Strange glamour, I have summoned.
Illusive like a butterfly it comes and goes,
but I keep calling it back –the odd treasures of
a misfit not yet concerned for the dollar sign.

When two gypsy misfits meet,
the song is sweet. The sun is high, and
the day is long. Sitting under a tree concerned
only for ·leasure, blue skies, and what their
next meal might be in an Indian summer.
Jangling guitars spicily pick and strum, and bands
of colorful friends are aptly banging on their drums.

Dionysian dreams of sensuality, intoxicants,
and music, played out in a Peter Pan band.
Where will this dreamer lead us –to Never-
Never-Land? Though do remember this,
my friends, when chasing butterflies...

... la vie bohème is most illusory, and
faint winged creatures oftimes die.

The Weight

Against a bright, white, holy canvas
of God's creation,
engineer of time and space,
the artist and the medium.
We paint.

Our dark silhouettes
give
take
love
hate
defile
etcetera,
flipping like pages
in quick succession.

BUT BEWARE,
there is a spoiler!

And when we reach the end
of this ever-rolling film,
the reels of our lives,
our souls our measured,
not by deeds,
but by these,
the greatest of human attributes,
our weight in LOVE and FAITH.

<u>Wings of Eagles</u>

Everything as seen from a high place above,
in an eagle's eye view, wanting not for position
or place for my God has uplifted me.
Higher and higher I climb.

Mighty winds of power escalate
Your winged creations like angels.
Eyes of glass, sailing, soaring,
wind roaring against my face under a
marbled sky. Nest on a mountain side,
mouths of babes opened wide,
waiting for their daily bread.

So, if I am with the Master, His Spirit in
my breast, and I should fly what you think
is too high, have no fear! I will be safe in the
luminous shadow and within the magnificent span
of the Creator's ineffably awesome wings.

New Creatures

I wish I could relate to you the way you wish
I would, speak to you the only way you seem
to understand. And sometimes I do in a secret
place inside. But I can't do that anymore.
I hold that communication sacred now.
I have been sealed by my first love, made
a virgin again. I have been restored.
I see no need to throw myself away.
Quick and easy evil, pleasure now, pay later
—desire, disease, death, heartbreak,
and new creatures —it's a sticky situation.

I want back the large piece of myself you stole
from me. I want to give back the few fragments
I stole from you. I can no longer deal in this cold
user's game. I was looking for the real –seeking.
I found it in Jesus. He is the most real thing I have
ever seen. Now, lend your ear to the Spirit speaking:

"Bring my children unto me early while they
still retain their innocence and do not yet know
the dark, drowning depths of Satan's snares,
nor let yourselves be defiled anymore.
Oh, sons and daughters! I want only for
the salvation and wellbeing of your souls.
I am not so concerned for your instant
gratification, rather that you be preserved
and entered into the Kingdom. The road
begins and extends from here. Be still,
and know that I am God. I LOVE YOU!"

Ride the Spirit

Calling all star trippers! Come, all you seekers!
Enter in lovers! Tell your fathers, your mothers,
your sisters, and brothers. Bring your broken,
your strange, the lost, and the weary. Come one,
come all, to the True Star –He, His Highness,
His Bright and Morning Majesty –the one, and
only Lord, Jesus Christ who bled for you!
I know you've been looking. I know you've
been searching, to fill the void, the vacuum inside.

When sin snowballs, collecting all sorts of sediment
on its way down –when the freedom you've known
and embraced starts spinning out of control and the
wild mare you ride is breaking, emptiness floods
in and you find yourself nowhere.

Come as you are! Love will not discriminate,
judge, or categorize. Just take His hand and
start walking. Taste and see that the Lord is good.
You'll never know until you try!

Don't concern yourself with all the big questions
right now. We'll never have all the answers
here anyways. Just ride the Spirit, the stealth stallion
He is. Hold on tight and go with flow! Try Him and
discover, His Spirit will carry, the angels will sing,
as you rise above your obstacles and sail into victory!

Treasure Bay

In my golden mansion, you leave small gifts
that have meaning only to me. You walk beside
me through lush gardens. We linger long on jeweled
shores collecting shells and semi-precious stones.
Sparkling waves lap our feet. The sun's rays warm
us and shine in our hair. Then we dine at the terrace
restaurant overlooking the bay.

In a shanty behind the estate, lives a contented
man who spends most of his time under the docks
and combing the shoreline in search of gems
and old coins. There he finds the occasional riches
washed upon these beaches that once offered
up an abundance of a long-lost treasure.
Every new moon he rides his bicycle to the near
by village and exchanges some of his finds for goods,
but he keeps the ones that are special to him.

Later, at the palace of burgundy and gold, my love
and I sit by a white hot, dancing fire and sip
effervescent wine of the same color. I am swept
away by desire and your love. Then we lay our heads
on satin pillows, pull up velvet covers, and dream
of jeweled shores glistening in the sun.

Joy of the Mountains

I could die here in this land I've come to love
and feel good about it. My spirit would just
bounce up off this earth and into the sun.

When I entered your lovely bounds,
you whispered hello with a rose and
decorated my hair with blackberries and lilac.

·Hear, the region's splendor, so much the eye to see.
From San Francisco to Vancouver the humpbacks
appear and ocean's home to Dungeness.

Fruited lands of redwood pines, rocky coastline,
country of wine. Ride the rails. See mysteries
revealing, to old northwestern underground cities.

Ancient volcanic mountain now filled to
unfathomed depths with resplendent,
sapphire waters –its shining, blue disc.

Snowcapped Shasta, caverns, mines, and
the steep, inclined ramps for runaway trucks of log
upon great rolling hills of light terracotta.

Fog and snow, haze of mist, and sunlight's shading,
ever painting, ever greens with brush of scented sage,
the holographic mountains that never look the same,
keeping company with clouds and
seasons ever changing.

Bear and salmon, desert, dunes,
and flower's rapturous joy to bloom...

... "She flies with her own wings," is the motto of state.
Oregano means, "joy of the mountains" in Greek.
Could this be how she claimed her name?

Your moods are so variable, moving across your
·featuresque face, offering your tears to the grower
and the growth, but mostly you smile.

Seuss trees with tip tops oddly curling,
furry topiaries and bushy bunches on arms of wiry,
bending branches, and sagging limbs of sloping
slanted, reach out like a grandfather's arms.

Molten lava and earthen flows have formed colossal
paws of lion and sphinx that align the great and wide
dividing river, sheeting like turquoise glass while steep
cliffs of hillside and pine rise to nested, privileged
windows, gleaming and boasting majestic
views on the other side.

Someday, I will be with God looking down.
I will be that happy face inside a warmly glowing sun.
Let the sun shine on. Let the winds blow on.
Let the birds sing on. My spirit will be smiling down
upon my loved ones and these lands I've come to love.

Inro: The Grabber

*Written during a time I suffered ten days with a rare, severe form
of depression called Anhedonia, being off my SSRI for six months.*

‡ There is a beast within us all that lies dormant just below the surface of all that is commonplace and pleasant. The Grabber prays on the weak. Sleeping with one eye opened, it waits patiently for a gap or an opening and a way in, for the barriers of our strength and defenses to fail. Once aroused, its ugly head peeks up from its resting place and curdles the very life blood coursing inside, setting the loins afire and the skin ablaze with fear. Then the claws appear, ready made to scratch at your sanity and lay hold your soul. In the rare instance the ghoul should triumph in its snatching, it will drag its victim kicking and screaming into the abyss where the gnashing is unceasing and the wailing without end. ‡

The Grabber

My pleasure juices are running dry.
Peace is hard to find and sleep's not coming easy.
I am wide awake. Even breathing seems an
arduous task. I try to breath smooth and shallow
as not to waken the crouching, ravenous beast inside.

Oh, No, I'm slipping! Help! It wants me!
It gets me in its grasp and I am scratched
and cut. I jump up to escape and reach for
something pleasant to soothe me. I look into

... the mirror and tell myself things are okay and
looking fine. Calm down I say, then start to
pray little rhymes I've been making
to chase my fears away.

Hard candy, some gum to chew might help,
an oral, tasty sweet. Maybe a rhythmic sound,
tick, tock, tick, tock, a metronome or a clock,
a heartbeat from the womb, something
to keep my mind from where it shouldn't be.
Music, a read, a walk, someone to talk to,
a candle lit, warm milk or tea, anything to get
a handle on this anxiety, for you see
when all pleasure dissipates, life is but
a black hole, and a man will self-destruct.

I take a mild sleep aid and begin to relax.
I've evaded the monster for now.
I lie back down in hopes I can make it to
·dreamland before it grabs me again.

Lyrics & Lullaby

Grandma's Little Prayer

Folk / Country

When I was just a young girl, my grandma said to me,
"Here's a little closing prayer that will handle
every need." Passed down from generations,
a treasured family jewel, a petition to our precious
Lord that covers every base for you.

Now, it may be short and simple, from the
Emerald Isles so green, but it holds a special message
that's meant for you and me. And it says:

"Dear Heavenly Father, keep me in a state of grace.
Deliver me from all evil, Lord, and shelter me
from sin and shame, from sin and shame.
Protect me from all accidents and illness,
and spare me an untimely or dishonorable death,
by Your wisdom and Your might within me, Lord,
through our Savior and Redeemer Jesus Christ."

Amen ...Hallelujah! ...Amen.
Amen ...Hallelujah! ...Amen.

Now, when we look to our Loving Father
for our protection and our needs, things seem
to take an upward turn, and cares leave on the breeze.
This is a vital lesson, one that we'd fair well to keep.
Take it with you to your dying day and there
the Lord you'll meet.

Way Down West
Folk / Country

I'm goin' to Arizona with a suitcase in my hand.
Hop aboard a Greyhound, take a good look at this land.
I'm leavin' all my old friends and my family.
I want to be my own boss and live a life that's free.

So, I'm going, going, gone... for the ones
who've done me wrong. Yes, I'm going, going,
gone, down the road.

Just have to change and rearrange the corners of my life.
'Cause this land I've been livin' in has cut me like a knife.
And Grandma's knitting me a scarf, funny thing, ya know?
'Cause I don't think I'll be needing it where I'm a gonna go.

Well, I'll make it in Arizona where the air is fresh and clean,
watch my skin turn brown in a sunny desert scene.
See your little desert queen livin' way out in the west.
Arizona or bust, goin' way down west.

Just have to go. Daddy, please don't cry, just have to go.
Just have to go. Mama don't ya know, just have to go.

I'm goin' to Arizona with a guitar on my back,
ride astride an iron horse, movin' down the tracks.
'Cause these dreams I've been wishin' on are takin' far too
long. And by the time you get to me, I'll have been long gone.

That's why I'm going, going, gone... for the ones
who've done me wrong. Yes, I'm going, going,
gone, down the road.

Just have to change and rearrange the colors of my life.
'Cause this land I've been livin' in has cut me like a knife.
And Grandma's knitting me a scarf, funny thing, ya know?
'Cause I don't think I'll be needing it where I'm a gonna go.

Yes, I'll make it in Arizona. Gonna let my spirit flow
where an eagle flies in a turquoise sky
and the prickly cactus grows.
See your little desert queen livin' way out in the west.
Arizona or bust, goin' way down west.

Just have to go. Daddy, please don't cry, just have to go.
Just had to leave. Baby, you'll miss me, just had to go.

And I hope someday you'll be my guest to
write or just drop by, see the tumbleweeds
and the Joshua trees, the eagles in the sky.
And I'll send you postcard of a feathered Indian chief.
See the terra cotta sands and a painted hut motif.

Just have to go. Mama don't ya know, just have to go.
Just had to leave. Baby, you'll miss me, just had to go.
Going, going, gone, down the road.
Down the road, there I go, down the road.

High on Grace
Soulful Folk / Country

I get high-igh-igh on Grace. When I look, I see Your face.
And You never let me down. I get high on Grace.
I get high-igh-igh on Grace. When I look, I see Your face.
An' I act just like a clown. I get high on Grace.

You embrace the children with Your Father's heart.
You are my everything. We'll never be apart.
You carry the pearl of hope in Your gentle hands.
Sent by the Master into the bitter lands.

And I get high-igh-igh on Grace. When I look, I see
Your face. And You never let me down. I get high on Grace.
I get high-igh-igh on Grace. When I look I see Your face.
An' I act just like a clown. I get high on Grace.

I hear Your footsteps movin' down the hall.
Their imprints follow You wherever You are called.
Looking for the answers, I listen for Your voice.
To love You, my Sweet Lord, I never had a choice.

You walk about the hallowed halls.
You're with the soldier when he falls.
Grace is there in what is right,
when a blind man gains his sight.
Sounding out in love's display,
Grace is there to save the day.

From up above, You come with love.
Come what may, there's always Grace.
There's always Grace.

That's why I'm high-igh-igh on Grace. When I look, I see
Your face. And You never let me down. I get high on Grace.
I get high-igh-igh on Grace. When I look, I Your face.
An' I act just like a clown. I get high on Grace.

Floating above the ground, silken robes aflow.
Sharing forgiveness falling like the snow.
You walk beside me. You are my best friend.
Stay with me Morning Star until the very end.

Grace is in the prison gates,
at the deathbed face to face.
Grace is in the hands that feed,
in the humble healer's deed.
Sounding out in love's display,
Grace is there to save the day.
From up above, You come with love.
Come what may, there's always Grace.
There's always Grace.

Yes, I get high-igh-igh on Grace. When I look, I see Your face.
An' I act just like a clown. And You'll always be around.
And You never let me down. I get high on, I get high on,
I get high on Graaace. I get high on Your inconceivably,
ever Amazing Graaace.

Old Man is Dead
Cadence / Field Song / Jazz

Old man is dead and in the ground. ...Hallelujah!
My old man is dead and in the ground. ...Amen!
Old man is dead and in the ground. ...Hallelujah!
My old man is dead and in the ground. ...Amen!

Dung is in the soil gonna raise some high cotton.
Dung is in the soil gonna raise it up high.
God Almighty's gonna raise me high cotton.
God Almighty's gonna raise it to the sky.

Jesus gonna give me some snow-white linens.
His angels gonna spin me a robe so white.
Jesus gonna give me some snow-white linens.
His angels gonna spin me a robe so white.

Old man is dead and in the ground. ...Hallelujah!
My old man is dead and in the ground. ...Amen!
Old man is dead and in the ground. ...Hallelujah!
My old man is dead and in the ground. ...Amen!

Playtime is Over

Lullaby

Playtime is over. Bedtime is here.
Time to lay your head down and rest my Dear.
Sleepy time, sweet dreams, sugar plum,
and wait for the morning sun to come.

When the sun comes up and the rooster crows,
we'll make our breakfast and blow our nose.
I'll make my coffee and (child's name) will play.
It's time for another livelong day.

And it will be a great day in the morning time,
great day in the afternoon, great day in the
evening time, great day whenever I'm with you.

And we'll live, live, live, the livelong daaay,
Yes, live, live, live, the livelong daaay.

But now I really need to tell you Darlin' that...
playtime is over, Honey. Bedtime is here.
Time to lay your head down and rest my Dear.
Sleepy time, sweet dream, sugar plum,
and wait for the morning sun to come.
Yes, wait for the morning sun to come.
We'll wait for the morning sun to come.

Beyond
part four

A Stone's Throw

Sometimes, a pebble tossed into a pond creates
a ripple that rolls out to its crusty edges,
touching the land and a few souls.

Sometimes, the stone's throw, by its sheer weight,
just sinks into the lake's foggy bottom.

But every now and again a boulder breaks the water's
surface with such intensity it causes a great swell.

The tsunami that ensues crashes the shoreline with
its tidal forces, blowing in doors, homes, and barriers;
smashing the windows of misconception and every
false notion and splintering their shelters like so much
straw; cleansing and correcting all it reaches of
delusion and untruth and turning on a light to the
genuine, and stirring many in a whirlpool of real as then
it splashes upon and sprinkles all flesh and every
wavelength in between.

Master Pillow

When I first saw you in the farmer's rustic backyard
shambles, your dark profile stood upon a wooden box,
not to look at me, but as an independent lookout
while gayer ones of parti and marigold stormed the
wire fence to yap at my feet. You were there keeping
watch or drawing attention to yourself in a sly way,
though the smallest one, already ten months old.
"Yes, I'll take the black one please."

Black, runt Pomeranian, shrunken sled dog of old,
five-pound bundle of joy, God's precious, created gift,
best friend to man and for me, the occasional purse traveler.

First afraid to walk the strange kitchen floor,
your claws frantically scurry and scratch, slipping and
going nowhere upon the waxy sheen like ice.
Warily testing the new surface, you finally
learned to negotiate ever so gingerly.

Timid in the early days, you've now come into
your own. Sweet one person devotional, barks and
growls to defend as if he perceives ownership of me
rather than I of him. He seems to say, "Keep Away!
This is my human!" You snort and scratch the rug like
a bull, hearing and alerting me to sounds my ears
don't comprehend.

... Late at night, I carry my infant to bed. Once reclined
he rushes in pursuit. Little tongue licks long the
interesting labyrinth of my ear in a sort
of interspecies communion. Then he rests
at my bosom, right there at my heart,
or off on his own behind me curled up and
leaning into the curve of my back in a small ball where
we slumber and sleep. As we waken, lounging on the
big pillow we call bed, tiny teeth playfully nip and bite,
causing nothing more than a pleasurable pressure
and tickling to my fingers while ceaselessly,
you rollover with your little doggy demands,
begging for your belly to be rubbed.

A natural nutcracker, he carries raw walnuts in
from the falling tree and chews out the oily meat.
Dear Mr. Pillow, my darling baby boy, your paws relax
and curl, and lazy lids meet in my embrace because
you trust me. Oh, such tiny paws and diminutive
turned up nose. You frolic and dance about me,
bouncing and panting, appearing to smile.

Down to the edges of the lovely blue-green river
known as Rogue, I toss him into three-foot waters
and under he goes. Tiny head bobs up emerging,
swimming back to me and the land. Long fur hides
long legs that petite frame reveals only when wet.
There he shakes off, and I pick up his shivering,
but he still loves from within his simply knowing,
that this is his lot in life, for his mistress shall do as
she pleases, and what a good mistress she is...

... Home again, now cozy and warm. Eyes so dark
set in sable fur, I search for glints of light that let
me know I'm in his sight. Yea, Mr. Pillow, beloved
little man-beast, would you ever grant entry another
true fellow, join me on the big pillow where you
often reside there amongst the other stuffed décor
that bear your namesake? Or will you drive
them all away with your high-pitched roar?

Ode to the Lizard King

Beautiful boy-man, lovely poet, troubadour, lost and
estranged from family who could never understand
the unfathomable depths of your true graces and
why you laid it all to waste.

Coy at first, young star, you performed with your
back to the audience, but once ignited, streaking tail,
you singed our hair and our minds with your reality.

You met your soulmate early, bound and entwined
with a flaming haired beauty, but chains not upon
your freedom to taste and drink from another's cup.

They say that fame is addicting, but doth not satisfy.
Living in the young lion's majestic lair, enthroned upon
the hungry alter proved too much to bear. So, you just
let it all go, hiding yourself behind a full Viking beard,
extra pounds, and bushy hair...

...You don't know me, dusky poet, but we are much the
same, to visit worlds unending created in your mind
and linger long the islands taken on the wings of time,
drifting down deep filled desert arroyos after the rain.

I would love to see you in heaven, wistful, wasteful,
wild child, meet and greet you in the air, but to be
quite frank, I have to wonder if you're there.
Yet, still I wish you would be in that great divine,
not lost; but that's not up to me now, is it?
That decision's with the Boss.

You left an odious mystery down along the King's
Highway. Did you stain your precious hands and throw
the Jack of Hearts away? Maybe it was something of
yourself you killed out there, sacrificing the flesh mask
to the real, upon your inner voyage of the vast mirage.

In a vote of confidence, bluesman, I don't believe
you did. The place was far too deep and wide where
you kept your secrets hid. I shed a large, iridescent
tear for you, lovely poet, troubadour. It falls into the
hands of God that only He and future's eye might see.

Painting by Peter Paul Rubens

The Dance

Did you know that every song longs to be heard,
every poem read? Every painting desires a place
on a wall? Every Ferris wheel wishes to be fared;
honey tasted, stars gazed upon? The flower says,
"Smell me." Every puppy says, "Pet me."
Somewhere, a dance wants to be performed.

And on and on the relations go like a partner's waltz,
a mental, emotional, and spiritual intercourse of the
senses, one to another; eyes to action and beauty;
ears to sound and music; tongue to flavor; touch to
texture; nose to scent; mind to matter, spirit to love.
All this, God's awesome love for us, His creation
creating; His experience experiencing,
all together and shared with Him.

Running Clouds

When we lie watching clouds drift by, is it they being
blown by the wind or we who are moving?
        ...Both perhaps.

This whirling, spherical ride is carrying us, right now,
the very place we are, 1037 miles per hour —faster than
most jet planes! Keeping us glued to the ground, so
fast, yet securely fastened to this great ship we don't
comprehend our traveling speed.

We rotate into night, rise up to day, and high-five the
sun on this giant, spinning orb, the lovely blue-green
marble we call home, ever evolving and revolving
around our star. So perfectly timed and
choreographed the waltz between mother
earth and her man, the moon, you never see his
dark side, only his bright and sometimes shy, sleepy mask.

Appearing on the watery horizon, I see a ship come
into view, coming closer, growing larger, until it's in
plain sight. From a high enough zenith or wide
enough vista one may witness the gentle,
sloping curve of the earth.

Billions of stars hang dazzling far from city lights.
The Milky Way looks like wisps of cloud.
Every night many fall with a streaking tail and we wish.

Aurora Borealis, Saturn's glistening rings, the many
moons of Jupiter and its gorgeous gas clouds —all this
glorious, dizzy spinning... when will it ever end?

Many a Shoes & Boots

Many a shoes with worn out soles and the adornments
of yesterday, hats and jewels in a multitude of hues,
not captured on silken screen.

Many a smile, wallowing away awhile, personal,
proud moments, blue and ugly ones too, some lost
or left out to rot, waxing and waning with the tides,
seen only in a torrent of memory swiftly moving.

Hot looks, boots with hooks, and free flowing
patterns, though not great of sparkle or bone
—a life not followed by a lens.

The Indian shy face turns his back to the flash and
walks away. He'll keep his spirit to himself today.
Another outdoorsman with a knapsack on his back
turns and thumbs his nose at the photographer.

Oh, the many a shoes and boots with taps on heels,
clickin' down the avenue, hunting bargain basement
deals. Now, out on the town in new fringed, buckskin boots
—stomp, slide, and spin, cool steppin' cross the dance
floor in an Indian dance.

Top hat, tomcat, floppy hat with a feather, surely these
boots have seen better weather. Brand spankin'
new Doc Martens marching to the beat, my militant
dandies, salute and say cheese! Hold that smile.
Now, you've got the knack. You'd look good in a gunny sack...

... The recorded history that remains may
be enjoyed. But Oh, the many a shoes and
boots, worn out, faded, and forgotten hues
–the kicks, lids, and regalia of days gone by.

Quintiku

Moon's eye peaks through passing cloud of starry night.
Knowing tiger, nose up to late breezes, ears turn at
rustling leaves. Transforming silver star falls from night sky,
a vision of dying long ago. Black pond sparkles. A fish jumps
for joy in air sounding splash. Her lover comes a creeping.
Stripes of glorious form, they meet.

Twin Sight

Misty arc of color,
hopeful sight of old,
its playful sunny band
adorns the sky.

Exotic hues on
powdered wing,
a favorite of ladies,
her child's awe,
come out to taste
the dew of daisies
once on her fair day
... a butterfly.

Life So Strange

In this, our second renaissance, the hands of time whirl
so quickly around the clock's face, like running clouds
in a timelapse and quicksand through an hourglass.

Every fifth year we've seen a century's worth of
change, from pee pots to microdots, and Clara Bow lips
to microchips. Victorian, nouveau, beatnik, hippy,
the boomers, gen X, and the screaming mimis,
now all lay reposed in an old crypt holding a rose.

Mine was a screwed-up generation, courtesy of Kinsey & Hef,
·demiangels shot out from a cannon like expressive,
naked dancers each striking a pose, then floating
down into gentle piles that now litter the sides of the
golden road of unlimited devotion.

Memories of days gone by, photos in black and white,
friends from the past and lovers bring a tear drop to
my eye. Remembering our young faces, once lived
in places, the gossamer ghosts of yesteryear and the
remains of social graces, colorful beads of old ideals,
and moments flash –cube, I hold dear.

Bridges crumble. Waters recede or rise.
Even untouched, virgin land changes itself over time.
Trees enlarge pushing up through the ground, shoving
earth aside in all directions and new vegetation takes hold.

The sights and circumstance of our beloved, aging
faces offer proof to the reality of the passage of time.
With every line and wrinkle, each silvery strand, every...

... stroke of the brush by God's hand, we stand back
in envy of what we use to be, until the day comes
to lie back down in our crib and die. All this aging
and changing, leading up to our eventual farewells,
unfolding with every new variation and each
solitary facet, all seems to me to be the single
most mysterious, surreal, sentimental,
and strange aspect of life.

Needles & Brick

I am ·interjected with needles from
my heart to the top of my head.
The words run through my veins
like some kind of secret serum, then
across the path of my eyes, and I write.

As I build these pages, these walls
of brick and stone, I move up and down
on a roped, window washer type scaffolding,
constructing passages of line and word
with the mortar of spirit and truth.

Sometimes, I move whole slabs to
another section or change out one single,
inferior stone, now swinging from page
to page like an acrobat on a trapeze.

I erect these buttresses and constructs,
the outer shells of rooms I live in, my shelter,
my building, my house, my home, that all began
to take shape on scratch paper many years ago.

My Geisha

Sun domed with merchant bags,
small stepping through town,
admiration abounds.

Black almond eye set
in curve of high, white cheek
and wisp of rose.

Bun —cushion for some pins,
Hairline —ocean meeting night sky
and blooms a bud red lips.

The Geisha sits on her feet,
back erect as bamboo,
now smiling as she pours you tea.

Perfect, pale stocking feet slip
into smooth wooden platforms,
making sound and designs on floor.

Drilled in grace and orient,
her shy, seductive dance
peeks from a fan.

Stiffened, layered patterns flow.
Groups of muscle flex.
Great is her pleasing.

Making music on strings,
she then recites Haiku.
Another artist softly sings.
Great is her reward.

Dog Dreams

What are a dog's dreams, lids half closed,
eyes rolled back, body twitching, breathing funny
and making noises? Are they chasing a rabbit?
–burying a bone? Who knows?

When the wide-eyed tiger hunts its prey or looks for
a mate, or simply lies basking in the noonday, African
sun, or under a tree for that little relief in the shade,
anticipating the next light breeze to pleasantly waft
 over its magnificent stripes –what is it thinking
    behind those gloriously made eyes?
        What are a tiger's thoughts?

How does an elephant feel on the run, huffing and
puffing in the dust, pounding the earth below in
a thunderous, raging stampede? What must their
hearts undergo when they see their loved ones lying
slaughtered, tusks hacked off as they stroke and
caress their dead with their trunk and wail a
 mournful cry, left for the scavengers to pick
  apart –first the big cats, then the hyenas,
    the jackals and buzzards?
        What are an elephant's emotions? ...

... Some people arrogantly proclaim, "We have dominion
over the animals. They are here for our pleasure
and our use." While there is some truth to these words
–we eat, we cover ourselves with their skins, we fashion
precious parts into jewels, ornaments, and tools
–the teeth, the horn, the bone. Sometimes we hunt
when populations impinge and their ultimate suffering
and starvation is inevitable. Still, we must look deeper
for the meaning.

What God gave us is an awesome gift and resource
as well as some of our greatest joys –a best friend and
loving companion, and a plethora other pleasing inter-
relationships. But He also charged us with a very
serious responsibility –a stewardship.
He commissioned us to *take care* of the creatures,
to *take care* of the earth, in the most humane and
respectful way possible, in order to preserve all
these wonderful affairs and interactions, so that
we might reverie and unendingly ponder...
Just *what are* a dog's dreams... a tiger's thoughts?
What are an elephant's emotions?

Sleepytime
Rhymes & Prayers

<u>Sleepytime Rhymes & Prayers</u>

Oh, good town's people snug in their beds,
drifting to slumber dreams dance in their heads.
-◆-
Jesus, wrap me in Your holy light.
Send all devils and demon to flight.
Give me peace and rest this night.
-◆-
Lord, take me. I want to go,
over Jordan where milk and honey flow,
explore the many rooms of Your mansions up above,
and fill me with Your awesome love!
-◆-
Just beneath is a place to go
when storms are tossing to and fro,
gently submerging down below
where peace and calm and serenity flow.
-◆-
Purring, Persian, palace pussy
on some puffy, purple pillows,
near a peacock in the poppies,
preening by the placid pond.
-◆-
Dreams, dreams, fancy dreams,
tell a tale of unknown themes.
Take me places yet unseen.
Dreams, dreams, fancy dreams,
reveal the heart and all its schemes.
-◆-
Sandman comes, traveling from afar
as you wish upon your star.
Making plans for a new day,
Mr. Sandy comes and steals you away.

The Reach

Jesus saves a drowning sinner.
Jesus sets the captive free.
He breaks the chains and rolls the stone,
unlocks the door and heals the wound.
Oh, how far reaching and deep diving,
the dark corners Your blood goes.

Firefly

Hands raised, we lift our praises and worship,
reaching out to lay hold and grasp within the
soul that elusive piece of God's radiance,
His Spirit. We open our hands to gaze at it
glowing in our palm like a firefly before it
quickly flits off into the hardened, brittle,
clay mask of this fallen, yet still beautiful world.
This side of the darkened veil for now,
a glimmer in His eye is all we may see.

Faith is not a product of reason, but of Spirit.
The great shining of His brilliance awaits he
who believes. Then we will see His glorious
light, no more a firefly in the night.
Behind the veil, His sights we'll see,
the splendors of His majesty.

Lord of All

All the water that flows,
The land and all that grows,
Our Creator made them all,
All the creatures great and small.
The sky and heavens up above,
He made them with His awesome love.

Sacred Stillness

In the sacred stillness of morning's early light,
Sins may be erected and brought unto our sight.
Heed the warning signposts.
Turn Right! Turn Right!

Elementary

You are you and I'm just me,
Living in the human family.
He is he and she is she,
Living in the human family.

They're just them and they are they,
Living in the light of a brand-new day.
We are we and they are them,
Living like you are my friend.

You are you and I am I.
Together we can reach the sky.
He is he and she is she.
Without each other we will surely die.

Beyond
part five

No More Dust

Dirt, dust, grime, grease, gunk, rust, rot, residue,
ruin –all this waste, debris, and decay, not to mention
the death. This is our world –where we live.
How would you like to live in a place where
there is none of this?

Here, we try to fix and cover over all things ugly,
taking comfort in the thought that nothing is perfect.
Everything exists wholly perfect only in its
absolute and perpetual imperfection.

In this other place I speak of, you need not ever clean
or dust, relieve yourself, nor bathe. The white glove
always passes the test. The food is beyond delectable
and the amenities to die for. You can eat whatever
your heart desires, anytime, and never gain an ounce.
The wine and song are always on tap, and we dance
and leap for joy with ever abounding jubilance
and praise. There will be no more tears or pain, only
laughter and exaltation. Breathtaking scenery rolls on
without end. The weather is always meek and mild.
And we adore Him, He who is responsible for this
lavish spread, the kind Landlord, the Proprietor,
the Host of Heaven, God Almighty.
Such peace and bliss in this world. So fresh and
sparkling immaculate, where the lion lies
down with the lamb forevermore.

Sila Señorita

Sila was a girl with sun in her smile. Her hair was the
color of sand. Her spirit seeking beauty wandered far
and wide the land.
Now, this Sila, this Sila was free,
she always was, and always will be,
not bound by ties of blood.
Once grown, she turned to face the big,
round world and asked, "Will you have me?"
"Yes, I will," said the big, round world.

Still learning, still seeking, she found herself in a land
bright and bursting with festive color. Where skins are
dark with sun kissed tan, she met a love, she met
a man. There her belly grew big and round like the
world, kicking with life inside. Filled with joy
to be a mother, she straddled the big wheel
and rode it twice over.

The household dealt in native crafts, of color, of
cotton, felt and leather. Surrounded with lovely
garments, she adorned herself and wore them well,
this blue-eyed lady fair,
in these lands of deep and brilliant color.
Yes, this Sila, this Sila is free,
she always was, and always will be,
not bound by ties of blood.

Once her children were grown, she turned to face
the big, round world and asked, "Will you keep me?"
"Yes, I will," said the big, round world...

... Back to the land from which she came, still learning,
   still seeking, still a mother, still a lover and a friend,
   and still marketing the items of tradition, she travels
   the world over capturing the beauty she sees
   through her lens. In the land from which she came
   there are great, ancient, rolling mountains. There she
   crouches like a puma perched high in an enclave,
   surveying her domain. Summer –green, autumn
   –colors, winter washes them white. When she feels
   the chill groan deep in her bones, she returns back
   to the land where her children were born.

The rest of her story is yet to be told, or at least as
   yet unknown. But one thing I believe upon her illusive
   capture on mental screen, in the end she will turn
   to face the big, round world once last time and ask...
   "Will you let me go?" "Yes, I will," the big, round
   world will reply. For you are Sila, and Sila is free,
   she always was, and always will be,
   not bound by ties of blood.

The Whipping Post

I do not wish to be a spectator mulling about
the captive crowd around the whipping post you
are tied to –ten lashes with a cat-o-nine tails.

I am not the masked executioner. I do not
aspire to light the fire that burns you to the stake
–opens the hatch –lets go the rope.

I do not desire to be a spider on the wall
of your inner sanctum of persecutions.

Lord knows, I've seen more than my share of
torment and torture, the condemnations, both real
and imagined. I've endured my whipping post,
my burning, my inquisition –more than you will
ever know. I am a descendant of Patriarchs d'Arc,
through one of Joan's brothers who were granted
the royal name "du Lys" meaning, "of Lily's" sometime
after her burning. Insanity perhaps... –a generational
curse running somewhere in the blood?

I am not your judge or jury. Nor do I require
a certain adulation –a host to sing my praises,
hail my name or worship at my feet.

Along the path of martyrdom minor, cast all pearls
to swine –orbs of illumination struck down by lesser
men who cover their eyes intimidated by the glow.

Hence, if I have sinned, I have failed –if I caused pain,
I am dealing with it now while I still have the chance.
I will take my licks upon the post again and again,
that I need not face them after death in a place of
partition, purging, penance, and pain –wherever or...

... whatever you say it is –or even *if* it is.
Even granted God's pardon, I will do my best
to be cleansed and wash my hands of the effects
of sin here and now, so that I may receive the
full glory of His graces.

If hell was below the surface of the ocean and had
many levels, as I believe it does... like the sea and
its levels, the first few feet down, on a bright day,
one could see the glimmering sunlight refracting
through the movement on the face like God's love
and hope showing through, it would warm you.
But further down less of the light could be seen,
less heat to feel, until there would be no light and
no warmth at all. Nothing... only cold and
darkness and the unknown scenes only that
much blackness could bring. Burning maybe...
–sixteen demons feeding on your soul?

Hell is a prison, a temporary holding place.
No one will be prayed out of hell! Only the
Great White Throne to be their release.

Therefore, my heart's greatest desire is to be
caught up with Him on that most awesome day.
At His trumpet's sounding, He will write a new
name upon my brow. I will reside in joyous,
ethereal mansions when the new heavens and
earth are spoken alive once again by His Word,
in a most unfathomably, magnificent display.
There, He will be our light without ceasing, and
there will be no more crying or pain. Suffer the
poor self-damned contained in the Lake of Fire.
For them, there is no way out. Amen.

Life is a Jungle

Life is a jungle and a treacherous trail. With our trusty
machete in hand, we cut through the brush and the
briers, swinging from side to side, chopping down
branches, fighting the whole way until finally,
we reach a clearing and it's free sailing once again.

Life is a jungle. Sometimes in the valley, sometimes in
the hill, we climb and climb to reach our destination
and finally come to rest on the summit. You can see
for miles an endless vista that seems to stretch on forever.

Life is a jungle. When you're in the thicket
wielding your sickle, sweat pours from your brow and
into your eyes. It's hard to see your way through.
It feels like an eternity till the rushes finally
spit you out at the other end.

Life is a jungle and a treacherous trail. With its ups and
downs, its tearing away, and expectations to prosper
along the path, what you lose in looks and curb appeal,
hopefully, you gain in wisdom and a steadfast stride.
The only thing I can tell you for sure is,
it will never end until we die.

Regret

Child, throw away your toys, your dark possessions,
the building blocks of babes that only tear down
in the playpen of your advisory –grief.

This space in not Mine, and not at all where I want
you to be! I am not the author of this confusion –pain!
Yet, think it not strange or mysterious. The wiles
of the dark prince go far beyond the pale.

Lay them under grave boards now –sealed.
Mark them with the symbols of the unknowable.
Remember My Sea of Forgetfulness. For you at
long last worship in Spirit and in Truth. You have
found the straight and narrow way and Oh, what
a glorious future to you belongs.

Let the light of your joy shine in great imbalance
to the darkness. Let My love envelope you, for all
provision is with you. Unlike the most foul and
deceptive symbol of the yin-yang –black dragon of old,
the light will overtake! You, my child, are not to be trodden.

The Inside Linemen

*A reflection on the most intense
period of my illness of youth.*

My mind, and painfully so, feels like an opened book,
a vast expanse of rolling, overturning treasures being
revealed, a brain to be picked by scavengers flying
overhead sent to burglarize my brain.

Joni. Maya. —You don't need my mine. The fluid
substance flows fully fermented, fragrant, and aged
by your wise, old souls before it ever hits the paper like fine
wine from a dusty bottle. So, you will leave mine —won't you?

I feel like nothing is really mine, not my thoughts,
not my dreams, my sights, nor sounds. All of it is
broadcast to anyone I take the slightest interest in,
let alone my major interests. They are with me all
the time, from within and without, in the
shower, in my mind.

They can hear me, but I not them. They can see
all of me, but I not them, only the thoughts
they wish to reveal and send.

My lover creates my dream stories then projects them
onto the screen of my mind. He does the audio and
the visual. He tinkers with my subconscious as I sleep.
When does he sleep, I wonder, for he is
always with me?

Aahh... do you smell this rose?
How do you like the song I'm listening to? ...

...When I cry, you feel the pain.
When I wash, you feel the warm water on my face.
When I change my clothes, you see me naked.
Do you really taste the tuna as I chew,
as it rolls across my tongue and down the tube?!

I Don't Chase the Butterfly

I don't chase the butterfly. I let it come to me.
The sky gives birth, and a galaxy is born. Tiny moons
  encircle the planets. Planets circle the stars glimmering
    like beaded sequins or wisps of rare gem on the train
      of His garment, His Majesty, the King of the universe.

The ·metamorphi lands and alights my consciousness.
What worlds will it bring me this time?
  What fertile seeds of insight will be planted there?
    What will it leave me today to share,
      some sights or sounds, an idea?

A translucent and fluid droplet from the sea, I hold
  in my cupped hands, floating just above like crystal.
    What does it contain to tell you of, some flavor,
      a concept, the scent of the ocean?

All I can say for certain is, there will surely be some
message there, if not just a feeling, some wave of
  emotion, a stitch of sorrow, a strand of illusion, or
    grain of truth, something to hold on to and remember.
      No, I no longer chase the butterfly.
        I let it come to me.

An Beag Paidir n'Cosaint
A Petite Prayer for Protection

Dear Heavenly Father,

¤

Keep me in a state of grace.

Deliver me from every evil.

Shelter me from sin, shame & scandal.

Protect me from all accidents & illness, and

Spare me an untimely or dishonorable death,

by Your wisdom & might within me, through

Our Savior & Redeemer Jesus Christ.

¤

Amen

Prayers of Night
A Poet's Prayers

-❋- Bless on the Morrow -❋-

<u>Adoni, I adore You,</u> for You are my provider, El Shaddai,
the God of more than enough. Thank You, Lord God,
for the blessings and gifts You have given me –pressed
down, shaken together, and running over, and poured
out from the windows and doors of heaven because
I am daily fed, Spirit led, and obedient to the Truth.
Thank You for strengthening and establishing me
and thank You for giving me Your wisdom.

<u>Dear Lord Jesus,</u> I adore You, Holy One of Israel.
How I love Your commands and Your grace.
Thank You my brave Lord for Your loving sacrifice
and victory over death and hell at the cross.
Cover me with Your precious holy blood.
Surround me in Your light and love.
Forgive me all my sins, known and unknown,
as I partake of the elements, Your most cherished,
miraculous blood and priceless holy body that was bruised
and striped for my forgiveness and ultimate healing.
By Your stripes I am healed and made whole.
I am Your body, bone of Your bone, flesh of Your flesh,
and blood of Your blood. We are blood brothers.
I am in You and You are in me in holy communion.

<u>Holy Spirit, I adore You.</u> Thank You for being
here and that You have never left me though there
were many times I caused You, not to turn, but to grieve…

...You are the power of God on earth.
You are the finger, the arm, and the muscle of God.
You are the doer, the action, and the activator of God.
You are Creator. You know me inside and out,
my every cell and sinew. Please keep me in
divine health. Your Word is health to my
flesh and strength to my bones.

You are my Father, Brother, King, Friend, and
Lover of my soul. In Your being I am made whole.
I am whole. I am able. I am safe. I am blessed.
I am cared for. I am loved. I am well.

—◆—

Lord, exalt Your true body in the evil end of days.
Send the world's wealth our way.
Set us in position. Give us recognition when the
light of Your radiance rises upon us like the sun.
Clothe us in Your righteousness.
Crown us with Your Truth.
Pour out Your Holy Spirit, so we can tell
Your story, bring many souls to Your saving grace
and many sons to glory, for the latter house shall
be overflowing and more exceedingly
abundant than the first.

Lead me and guide me through to the last days
in strength. Sanctify me and burn up the dross.
Uphold me in prosperity and divine health as
You carry me through to the glorification and rapture
to receive my full inheritance which is the utmost desire
of my life and heart. How I long to see myself changed...

...in a mirror when I am, at last, separated from the evil
influence and receive the fullness of Your joy that
will be everywhere we look and rounding
every corner without fear.

—◆—

Thank You for the glorification, Lord, and thank you
for the Forty Days of Glory when You stop
time, and we, with the awesome help of Your Spirit,
will heal and prepare the people for what is to come.
Thank You for the splendorous rapture at the
trumpet's blast, which is Your voice's call, when we
are carried up into Your loving arms and behold
Your true beauty for the first time.

Thank You for Your Judgment Seat, Lord, when You
will burn away the remaining dross that I may
receive my rank and reward.

Thank You for my soldierly training, that we may
ride back with You to fight Armageddon and eliminate
the wicked and the damned from the world. You will
restore the earth to its former glory and more. You will rule
and rein over it with a gilded, gem encrusted rod of iron
and a heart full of love. And Lord,
thank You for our horses.

Thank You for the indescribably joyous and festive
Wedding Supper of The Lamb when we will celebrate with
You and the brethren, our numerous fine friends who share in
this Like Precious Faith. We alone, the intimate members of
Your Holy Body, all moving and working together...

...like intricate clockwork with You at the Head. We are
the Wheels within Wheels and the Sea of Glass.

<u>Thank You</u> for our long-awaited triumphal entry
into the city, our beautiful bride, Beulah, the New
Jerusalem where we will be pillars –Kings and Priests
for You in Your throne room. We will abide *in* and be
permanently fused *with* Your most exquisite of creations,
for You are both Creator and the Creation.
We will rule and rein with You over the Nations in
pleasures forevermore.

—♦—

For now, as I am an alien in this world, I will clothe
myself in Your full amour. First and foremost,
the <u>Buckle of Truth</u>, I gird about my loins. Your Truth,
I esteem above all else, for without it, one has nothing.
It is center, and to what all the other midsection armor
and weaponry is attached, barring helmet and boots.

I don the <u>Helmet of Salvation</u> that keeps me from
worry and torment and all false doctrines, for there is no
Love in Lie, and all lies and sufferings are from the devil.

I place the <u>Breastplate of Righteousness</u> over my
heart, for I am the righteousness of God in Christ Jesus.

I wield the fearsome, two-edged <u>Sword of the Spirit</u>
that is sharper than any two mouthed sword and speaks
truth into the universe. For when I speak Your Word
in faith, my enemies, which are foul spirits, are scattered
and smitten straight down the middle before
they ever near my face...

...I uphold the mighty <u>Shield of Faith</u> which stands
from head to toe and turns in all directions to quench
every fiery dart of the evil one. The Holy Spirit
is my rearguard and He protects my back.

And finally, my cleated and spiked <u>Fighting Boots</u>
are shined and gleaming with the preparation of the
Gospel of Peace. With all this, I stand at the ready,
in season and out, to uphold and act upon Your Truth
at a moment's notice and at every opportunity.

—◆—

You will perfect that which concerns me this day.
You will contend with that which contends with me
and You will save our children. Send out the convicting
Hound of Heaven, which is Your Spirit, after our
children and loved ones. Send laborers to cultivate
Your Word in their hearts. Lord, let not any of my
beloveds suffer in the Lake of Fire. Grant myself and
my loved ones a good, expedient, and pain-free death
should You terry beyond our usefulness. Yea, Lord,
please come quickly. We long to be with You, to see
Your face, and to see all things made right. Place Your
angelic forces around the perimeter of my property
to protect my home and belongings. Place them at
the four corners of my mind and heart to guard
and guide me into safe and peaceful slumber
unbothered by demonic dreams.

Peak to peak, glory to glory, strength to strength,
faith to faith, better to better, and success to success
—that's my life in You Lord! Higher and higher
I climb, ever transforming into your likeness...

As I navigate Your Narrow Way, straight
as an arrow –my face is set as a flint affixed
towards You and Your purpose.

—◆—

Teach me to Trust. Learn me Your Love.
Perfect Your Peace within me.

—◆—

<u>Lord, Bless on the Morrow</u>.
Hide me in Your lovely, garden pavilion;
safe within the folds of Your splendiferous robe;
snug in the feathers of Your mighty, majestic wings,
and high atop Your Strong Tower where the view
is good of my enemies and everything
as far as the Spirit can see.

Amen.

—◆—

Author † Poet

Lawren DeLass